SURRENDER

A Guide for Prayer

Jacqueline Syrup Bergan
and
S. Marie Schwan, CSJ

D1244813

Take and Receive Series

Revised and Updated Edition

theWORD among us® press

The Word Among Us Press
9639 Doctor Perry Road
Ijamsville, Maryland 21754
www.wordamongus.org

10 09 08 07 06   1 2 3 4 5

ISBN 10: 1-59325-084-3
ISBN 13: 978-1-59325-084-3

Made and printed in the United States of America

Library of Congress Control Number: 2006929677

Contents

Week One – Prayer of Love and Praise

Week Two – If Anyone Wants to Be a Follower of Mine

Week Three – The Soldiers Twisted Some Thorns into a Crown

Week Four – Today You Will Be with Me in Paradise

Week Five – My God, My God, Why Have You Forsaken Me?

Week Six – Into Your Hands I Commend My Spirit

Cover Design

*For now the winter is past,
the rain is over and gone.
The flowers appear on the earth;
the time of singing has come,
and the voice of the turtledove
is heard in our land.*
Song of Songs 2:11-12

"The time of singing has come." Throughout the church is heard the murmur of prayer. Quietly, and in stillness, within the hearts of Christians everywhere, winter has given way to the vitality of spring—the coming of the Spirit.

Among the heralds of spring are the return and nesting of birds. From the days of ancient Israel even to our own times, birds have been symbolic, not only of our deep homing instincts but also of our creative impulse and of our desire for transcendence.

Frequent allusions to doves are made throughout the Scriptures. In the Song of Songs, the dove announces spring; in Genesis, the olive-bearing dove indicates the end of the flood (Genesis 8:11). At the baptism of Jesus, the presence of the dove initiates a new age of the Spirit (Mark 1:10).

The mourning dove calls:
Arise, my love . . . for now the winter is past.
Song of Songs 2:10-11

The cover was designed by Donna Pierce Campbell, a popular Minnesota artist. Its beauty and freshness of style mirror the spirit of renewal that this guide for prayer hopes to serve.

Foreword

There was a time when "prayer" meant saying our prayers, and when "going on retreat" was reserved for priests and religious—and sometimes for students in high school or college. But quietly through the years, men and women of every age and state have heard and appropriated the blessed message that all men and women are called to holiness (Vatican II, *Lumen Gentium*). We have also learned that standing right with God, with others, and with ourselves, and that drawing closer to and walking each day with the incarnate and risen Lord, become possible for all who try to pray. Such a privilege is for each of us who listen and respond to God speaking through the Word and present in our midst. "Teach me to pray" is every disciple's petition.

Holiness begins with God and ends in God. God's love is everlasting, an active love manifesting itself in works of creation and salvation, fully revealed in the person and works of Jesus the Lord, and completed in his death. His love leads us to a life that will never end. Love reaches its fulfillment when it is returned, when it really becomes a mutual exchange of gifts. Realizing God's love is at the heart of our listening. Responding to the challenge, we love in return. This is the heart of our prayer.

Surrender: A Guide for Prayer, the fourth volume of the Take and Receive series, is a blessing for all those who want to pray, alone and with others. This book is an invitation to listen and respond to the Lord in the many ways it clearly and beautifully presents to us. God is good in bringing forth for those who search for a life of prayer books like these, which help all of us respond to the universal call to holiness.

Richard F. McCaslin, SJ
Superior, Creighton Prep Community
Omaha, Nebraska

To my brother
Allen William Syrup

To my sister
Michaela Syrup Key
—Jackie

To my brother
John Jerome Schwan
—Marie

Think of the love
that the Father-Mother
have lavished on us
by letting us be called God's children.
—1 John 3:1 (adapted)

Introduction

As a young military captain recovering from a serious battle wound, St. Ignatius of Loyola experienced a profound conversion. His insight into the human condition, combined with his personal knowledge of God's love, made him a master spiritual director. Eventually he wrote his Spiritual Exercises, through which millions of people would come to experience God's overwhelming and unconditional love for them. By praying through the Spiritual Exercises, Christians over four centuries have strengthened their commitment to live for the "praise of God's glory."

Like the other books in the Take and Receive series, *Surrender: A Guide for Prayer* is modeled on this great treasure of Christian spirituality. In this fourth of the five-volume series, experienced retreat leaders Jacqueline Syrup Bergan and Sr. Marie Schwan guide readers through thirty-six meditations (six per week) based on the second week of the Spiritual Exercises, incorporating key exercises of St. Ignatius such as the "Two Standards" and the "Three Kinds of Persons."

While modeled on the Spiritual Exercises, the guides in the Take and Receive series are neither a commentary on St. Ignatius' work nor are they designed to *be* the exercises. Instead, for each of the thirty-six days, Scripture passages are paired with incisive commentary and suggested prayer exercises, all of which are designed to help the user develop a more intimate relationship with the Lord.

The first volume, *Love: A Guide for Prayer*, makes use of the themes present in the "Principles and Foundation" of the Spiritual Exercises. We are led to realize that we are created in God's love, are totally dependent on that love, and are called to respond in freedom to praise, reverence, and serve God.

The second volume, *Forgiveness*, correlates with the first week of the Spiritual Exercises. As we move through the meditations, we become aware of the sin in our life and how it has become an obstacle to receiving God's love. Sin and sinner are considered in the light of God's merciful and forgiving love.

In the third volume, *Birth*, we are invited to contemplate the earthly life of Jesus from his incarnation through his public life. As we meditate on the deep meaning of Jesus' birth, his call, and his outreach to those in need, we grow in appreciation for the wonder of God entering so fully into our human condition. We experience, stirring within ourselves, the call of grace to respond decisively to that longing, placed deep within our hearts by the Holy Spirit, to know Jesus, to love him, and to follow him. Jesus truly becomes the way, the truth, and the life of those who enter into discipleship with him.

Volume four, *Surrender*, focuses on Christ's total submission to the will of God. Through the contemplation of Jesus' passion and death, we are led to an awareness of how suffering can be utilized and transformed. The consideration of paradox is especially significant; in the light of the cross, we encounter seemingly contradictory elements of our lives, which lead us to a new level of truth and integration. The prayerful use of this guide will lead to the discovery of how, in and with Christ, personal surrender to suffering is a labor of love as well as the way to a powerful union with God and with each other.

The authors wrote the Take and Receive series after discovering that people attending their workshops needed and desired more support in developing a personal relationship with God. Since that time, the guides have been a popular and enduring resource, both for spiritual directors and retreat leaders, and for all those men and women who have used them individually for personal prayer. While designed for solitary prayer, the guides can also be used for faith-sharing in small groups.

The Word Among Us Press is pleased to make available this new and updated edition. We pray that those who use this guide will satisfy the hunger for God that the Holy Spirit has planted in their hearts. May these meditations lead people, by the Spirit of Jesus, into true spiritual freedom.

The Word Among Us Press

Getting Started: How to Pray

Lord, teach us to pray. (Luke 11:1)

Prayer is our personal response to God's presence. Just as Jesus was present to his first disciples, so God is present to each of us every day. Therefore, we can approach him reverently with a listening heart. He speaks first to us. In prayer, we acknowledge his presence, and in gratitude, respond to him in love. The focus is always on God and what he does. The following suggestions are offered as ways to help us be attentive to God's word and respond to it uniquely.

Daily Pattern of Prayer

For each period of prayer, use the following pattern:

Before Prayer—Preparation. Plan to spend at least twenty minutes to one hour in prayer daily. Although there is nothing "sacred" about sixty minutes, most people find that an hour better provides for quieting themselves and entering fully into the Scripture passage. To better prepare your heart and mind, take time the evening before to read the commentary as well as the Scripture passage for the following day. Just before falling asleep, recall the Scripture passage.

During Prayer—Structuring Your Time. As you begin your prayer time, quiet yourself; be still inside and out. Relax and breathe in and out, deeply and slowly. Repeat several times.

Realize that you are nothing without God, and declare your dependency on him. Ask him for the grace you want and need. Then read and reflect on your chosen Scripture passage, using the appropriate form, such as meditation for poetic and non-story passages or contemplation for stories or events. (See the section at right on the variety of ways to pray privately.) Close the prayer period with a time of conversation with Jesus and his Father. Speak to God personally and listen attentively. Conclude with an Our Father.

After Prayer—Review. At the conclusion of the prayer period, take the time for review and reflection. The purpose of the review is to heighten your awareness of how God has been present to you during the prayer period. The review focuses primarily on what St. Ignatius described as the interior movements of consolation and desolation as they are revealed in your feelings of joy, peace, sadness, fear, ambivalence, anger, or any other emotion.

Often it is in the review that we become aware of how God has responded to our request for a particular grace or what he may have said to us. Writing the review provides for personal accountability, and is a precious record of our spiritual journey. To write the review is a step toward knowing ourselves as God sees us.

In the absence of a spiritual director or spiritual companion, writing the review helps fill the need for evaluation and clarification. If you have a spiritual director, the written review offers an excellent means of preparing to share your prayer experience.

Keep a notebook or journal with you during prayer. After each prayer period, indicate the date and the Scripture passage that was the subject of your reflection. Then answer each of the following questions: Was there any word or phrase that particularly struck you? How did you feel? Were you peaceful? Loving? Trusting? Sad? Discouraged? What do these feelings say to you? How are you more aware of God's presence? Is there some point to which you should return in your next prayer period?

A Variety of Ways to Pray Privately

There are various forms of scriptural prayer. Different forms appeal to different people. Eventually, by trying various methods, we become adept at using approaches that are appropriate to particular passages and are in harmony with our personality and needs. This guide will make use of the following forms:

1. Meditation

In meditation one approaches the Scripture passage like a love letter. This approach is especially helpful in praying poetic passages.

To use this method, read the passage slowly, aloud or in a whisper, savoring the words and letting them wash over you. Stay with the words that especially catch your attention; absorb them the way the thirsty earth receives the rain. Keep repeating a word or phrase, becoming aware of God's presence and the feelings you experience.

Read and reread the passage lovingly, as you would a letter from a dear friend, or as you would softly sing the chorus of a song.

2. Contemplation

In contemplation, we enter into a life event or story passage of Scripture. We enter into the passage by way of imagination, making use of all our senses.

Theologians tell us that through contemplation we are able to "recall and be present at the mysteries of Christ's life" (26, p. 149).* The Spirit of Jesus, present within us through baptism, teaches us, just as Jesus taught the apostles. The Spirit recalls and enlivens the particular mystery into which we enter through prayer. As in the Eucharist the risen Jesus makes present the paschal mystery, in contemplation he brings forth the particular event we are contemplating and presents himself within that mystery.

---

* Numbers are keyed to the Bibliography, pp. 171–175.

God allows us to imagine ourselves present in a specific Scripture passage, where we can encounter Jesus face to face.

To use this method, enter the story as if you were there. Watch what happens; listen to what is being said. Become part of the story, assuming the role of one of the participants. Then look at each of the individuals. What does he or she experience? To whom does each one speak? Ask yourself, "What difference does it make for my life, for my family, for society, if I hear the message?"

In the gospel stories, be sure to enter into dialogue with Jesus. Be *there* with him and for him. *Want him*; hunger for him. *Listen* to him. Let *him* be for you what he wants to be. *Respond to him.*

3. Centering Prayer

The Cistercian monk and writer M. Basil Pennington noted, "In centering prayer we go beyond thought and image, beyond the senses and the rational mind to that center of our being where God is working a wonderful work" (59, p. 18).

Centering prayer is a very simple, pure form of prayer, frequently without words. It is a path toward contemplative prayer, an opening of our hearts to the Spirit dwelling within us. In centering prayer, we travel down into the deepest center of ourselves. It is the point of stillness within us where we most experience being created by a loving God who is breathing life into us.

To enter into centering prayer requires a recognition of our dependence on God and a surrender to his Spirit of love. "Likewise the Spirit helps us in our weakness. . . . That very Spirit intercedes with sighs too deep for words" (Romans 8:26). The Spirit of Jesus within us cries out, "Abba! Father!" (8:15).

To use this method, sit quietly, comfortable and relaxed. Rest within your longing and desire for God. Move to the center within your deepest self. This movement can be facilitated by imagining yourself slowly descending in an elevator, walking down flights of stairs, descending a mountain, or going down into the water, as in a deep pool.

In the stillness, become aware of God's presence. "Be still, and know that I am God!" (Psalm 46:10). Peacefully absorb his love.

4. Repeated Prayer

One means of centering prayer is the use of a repeated prayer. It can be a single word or a phrase. It may be a line from Scripture or one that arises spontaneously from within your heart. The word or phrase represents, for you, the fullness of God. Variations of the prayer may include the name "Jesus" or what is known as the Jesus Prayer: "Lord, Jesus Christ, Son of God, have mercy on me, a sinner."

To use this method, repeat the word or phrase slowly within yourself in harmony with your breathing. For example, the first part of the Jesus Prayer is said while inhaling, the second half while exhaling.

5. Meditative Reading

"So I opened my mouth, and he gave me the scroll to eat. He said . . . eat this scroll that I give you and fill your stomach with it. Then I ate it; and in my mouth it was as sweet as honey."   —Ezekiel 3:2-3

One of the approaches to prayer is a reflective reading of Scripture or other spiritual writings. Spiritual reading is always enriching to our life of prayer, but is especially helpful in times when prayer is difficult or dry.

To use this method, read slowly, pausing periodically to allow the words and phrases to become part of you. When a thought resonates deeply, stay with it, allowing the fullness of it to penetrate your being. Relish the word received. Respond authentically and spontaneously, as in a dialogue.

6. Journaling

"The mystery was made known to me . . . as I wrote, . . . a reading of which will enable you to perceive my understanding of the mystery of Christ."

—Ephesians 3:3-4

Journaling is meditative writing. When we place pen on paper, spirit and body cooperate to release our true selves. There is a difference between journaling and keeping a journal. To journal is not merely to keep a record of events or experiences. Rather, it is to experience God's presence as we see ourselves in a new light and as fresh images rise to the surface from deep within. Journaling requires putting aside preconceived ideas and control.

Meditative writing is like writing a letter to one we love. Memories are recalled, convictions are clarified, and affections well up within us. In writing we may discover that emotions are intensified and prolonged.

Because of this, journaling can also help to identify and heal hidden feelings such as anger, fear, and resentment. When we write to God honestly, he can begin to heal past hurts or memories that have stayed with us for years. In addition, journaling can give us a deeper appreciation for the written word as we encounter it in Scripture.

There are many variations for the use of journaling in prayer. Among them are the following:

a. Writing a letter addressed to God.

b. Writing a conversation between oneself and another; the other may be Jesus or another significant person. The dialogue can also be with an event, an experience, or a value. For example, death, separation, or wisdom receive personal attributes, and each is imagined as a person with whom one enters into conversation.

c. Writing an answer to a question, such as, "What do you want me to do for you?" (Mark 10:51) or "Why are you weeping?" (John 20:15).

d. Allowing Jesus or another person in Scripture to "speak" to us through the pen.

7. Repetition

"I will remain quietly meditating upon the point in which I have found what I desire without any eagerness to go on till I have been satisfied."

—St. Ignatius of Loyola (72, p. 110)

Repetition is the return to a previous period of prayer for the purpose of allowing the movements of God to deepen within one's heart. Through repetition, we fine-tune our sensitivities to God and to how he speaks in our prayer and within our life circumstances. The prayer of repetition teaches us to understand who we are in light of how God sees us and who God is revealing himself to be for us.

Repetition is a way of honoring God's word to us in the earlier prayer period. It is recalling and pondering an earlier conversation with one we love. It is as if we say to God, "Tell me that again; what did I hear you saying?" In this follow-up conversation or repetition, we open ourselves to a healing presence that often transforms whatever sadness and confusion may have been experienced in the first prayer.

In repetitions, not only is the consolation (joy, warmth, peace) deepened, but the desolation (pain, sadness, confusion) is frequently brought to a new level of understanding and acceptance within God's plan for us.

To use this method, select a period of prayer to repeat in which you have experienced a significant feeling of joy, sadness, or confusion. You might also select a period in which nothing seemed to happen—due perhaps to your lack of readiness at the time.

To begin, recall the feelings of the first period of prayer. Use as a point of entry the scene, word, or feeling that was previously most significant. Allow the Spirit to direct the inner movements of your heart during this time of prayer.

Five Spiritual Practices and Helps

1. Examen of Consciousness

"O LORD, you have searched me and known me."   —Psalm 139:1

The examen of consciousness is the instrument by which we discover how God has been present to us and how we have responded to his presence through the day. St. Ignatius believed this practice was so important that, in the event it was impossible to have a formal prayer period, it would sustain one's vital link with God.

The examen of consciousness is not to be confused with an examination of conscience, in which penitents are concerned with their failures. It is, rather, an exploration of how God is present within the events, circumstances, and feelings of our daily lives. What the review is to the prayer period, the examen is to our daily life. The daily discipline of an authentic practice of the examen brings about a balance that is essential for growth in relationship to God, to self, and to others. The method reflects the "dynamic movement of personal love: what we always want to say to a person whom we truly love in the order in which we want to say it . . . Thank you . . . Help me . . . I love you . . . I'm sorry . . . Be with me" (18, pp. 34–35).

The following prayer is a suggested approach to the examen. The written response can be incorporated into the prayer journal:

> • God, my Father, I am totally dependent on you. Everything is a gift from you. *All is gift.* I give you thanks and praise for the gifts of this day.

> • Lord, I believe you work through and in time to reveal me to myself. Please give me an increased awareness of how you are guiding and shaping my life, as well as a more sensitive awareness of the obstacles I put in your way.

- You have been present in my life today. Be near, now, as I reflect on
  —your presence in the *events* of today;
  —your presence in the *feelings* I experienced today;
  —your *call* to me;
  —my *response* to you.

- Father, I ask your loving forgiveness and healing. The particular event of this day that I most want healed is . . .

- Filled with hope and a firm belief in your love and power, I entrust myself to your care, and strongly affirm . . . (Claim the gift you most desire, most need; believe that God desires to give you that gift.)

2. Faith Sharing

"For where two or three are gathered in my name, I am there among them."   —Matthew 18:20

In the creation of community, it is essential that members communicate intimately with each other about the core issues of their lives. For the Christian, this is faith sharing, and it is an extension of daily solitary prayer.

A faith-sharing group, whether part of a parish, lay movement, or diocesan program, is not a discussion group or social gathering. Members do not come together to share and receive intellectual or theological insights. Nor is the purpose of faith sharing the accomplishment of some predetermined task.

Instead, the purpose is to listen and to be open to God as he continues to reveal himself in the church community represented in the small group that comes together in his name. The fruit of faith sharing is the "building up" of the church, the body of Christ (Ephesians 4:12).

The approach of faith sharing is one of reading and reflecting together on the word of God. Faith sharing calls us to share with each other, from deep within our hearts, what it means to be a follower of Christ in our world today. To authentically enter into faith sharing is to come to know and love one another in Christ, whose Spirit is the bonding force of community.

An image that faith-sharing groups may find helpful is that of a pool into which pebbles are dropped. The group gathers in a circle around a pool. Like a pebble being gently dropped into the water, each one offers a reflection—his or her "word" from God. In the shared silence, each offering is received. As the water ripples in concentric circles toward the outer reaches of the pool, so too this word enlarges and embraces, in love, each member of the circle.

Faith-sharing groups are usually made up of seven to ten members who gather at a prearranged time and place. One member designated as the leader calls the group to prayer and invites them to some moments of silence, during which they pray for the presence of the Holy Spirit. The leader gathers their silent prayer in an opening prayer, spontaneous or prepared.

One of the members reads a previously chosen Scripture passage on which participants have spent some time in solitary prayer. A period of silence follows each reading of Scripture. Then the leader invites each one to share a word or phrase from the reading. Another member rereads the passage; this is followed by a time of silence.

The leader invites willing members to share how this passage personally affects them—whether, for example, it challenges, comforts, or inspires them.

Again the passage is read. Members are invited to offer their spontaneous prayers to the Lord. Finally, the leader draws the time of faith sharing to a close with a prayer, a blessing, an Our Father, or a hymn. Before the group disbands, the passage for the following session is announced.

3. The Role of Imagination in Prayer

Imagination is our power of memory and recall that makes it possible for us to enter into the experience of the past and to create the future. Through images we are able to touch the center of who we are and to give life and expression to the innermost levels of our being.

The use of images is important to our development, both spiritually and psychologically. Images simultaneously reveal multiple levels of meaning and are therefore symbolic of a deeper reality. Through the structured use of active imagination, we release the hidden energy and potential to become the complete person that God has created us to be.

When active imagination is used in the context of prayer, and *with an attitude of faith*, we open ourselves to the power and mystery of God's transforming presence within us. Because Scripture is, for the most part, a collection of stories rich in sensual imagery, the use of active imagination in praying Scripture is particularly enriching. When we rely on images as we read Scripture, we go beyond the truth of history to discover the truth of the mystery of God's creative word in our lives (22, p. 76).

4. Coping with Distractions

It is important not to become overly concerned or discouraged by distractions during prayer. Simply put them aside and return to your prayer material. If and when a distraction persists, it may be a call to attend prayerfully to the object of distraction. For example, it would not be surprising if an unresolved conflict continues to surface until you have dealt with it.

5. Colloquy: Closing Conversational Prayer

St. Ignatius is very sensitive to the depth of feeling aroused by the contemplation of the suffering of Jesus. While a suggestion for a conversational prayer has been provided at the end of each prayer period, you are encouraged to let your heart speak in an intimate outpouring of feeling, of love and compassion. You should attempt to be with Jesus in his suffering. Sometimes the closing conversational prayer will provide an opportunity to pour out feelings of discouragement, temptation, or fear or to express difficulty in entering into the suffering of Christ. It may even be necessary to pray for the desire to experience suffering with Christ. The important thing to remember is that simple presence is what is most important. Just to be silent in the presence of Christ's suffering is profound prayer.

Prayer of Love and Praise

Prayer of Love and Praise

Lord my God,
when Your love spilled over into creation
You thought of me,

I am
  from love
  of love
  for love.

Let my heart, O God, always
  recognize,
  cherish,
  and enjoy your goodness in all of creation.

Direct all that is me toward your praise;
Teach me reverence for every person, all things.
Energize me in your service.

Lord God,
May nothing ever distract me from your love . . .
Neither health nor sickness
  wealth nor poverty
    honor nor dishonor
    long life nor short life.

May I never seek nor choose to be other
  than You intend or wish.
Amen.

Week One, Day 1 | The Power and the Possibility

Luke 9:23-27

> *Then he said to them all, "If any want to become my followers, let them deny themselves and take up their cross daily and follow me. For those who want to save their life will lose it, and those who lose their life for my sake will save it. What does it profit them if they gain the whole world, but lose or forfeit themselves? Those who are ashamed of me and of my words, of them the Son of Man will be ashamed when he comes in his glory and the glory of the Father and of the holy angels. But truly I tell you, there are some standing here who will not taste death before they see the kingdom of God."*

Commentary

"I'll never forget the first time I heard that the resurrection of Jesus was to be experienced *now*, in the present," a friend shared. "It was a moment of heightened realization when suddenly, in a new way, I grasped the power and the possibility of the risen Christ within me. For days I walked in stunned awareness, knowing that I need not wait until death to experience the wonder of his spirit."

This reality of Jesus risen is the most astounding gift a loving Creator could give his human creatures. And we, as postresurrection people, find in Jesus risen the power and direction for our lives.

Luke's instruction to the early Christian community on discipleship must be read within the context of this living awareness of the resurrection. In

Jesus' own words, Luke imparts to us the heart and mind we too must nurture if we are to become authentic disciples of Christ.

Jesus presents us with a demanding challenge. He insists on unwavering loyalty. No one, no thing—no circumstance, embarrassment, or shame—can be allowed to deflect us from the priority of following him. And, not just some but *all* are called! By virtue of our baptism, each of us is invited to become Jesus' disciple.

Yet, within this unrelenting call is freedom of choice. Our choice is undeniably mirrored in our response to the simple question, *"How have I loved?"* The answer will reveal whether our journey has been self- or other-centered. In our seeking to find our truest selves, have our efforts and activities been directed primarily toward self-enhancement and security, or has our journey toward wholeness led us to an active, loving concern for others?

Luke presents us with "the most fundamental paradox of Jesus' teaching: that a life bent on personal survival is a life lost," but a life given in loving service is a life saved (43, p. 132). To say yes to this call to discipleship is to commit oneself to a complete orientation to the way of Christ. To follow Christ is to embrace life in its totality with all its joys, successes, failures, and disappointments; it is to concretely and daily encounter life's ambiguities, tensions, and paradoxes. To be a disciple of Christ is to courageously risk a sensitive and open response to the rhythm of light and darkness as it moves and shapes the reality of our lives.

Jesus says, "If any want to become my followers, let them deny themselves and take up their cross and follow me" (Matthew 16:24). The gospel invites us to assume our *own* cross as the circumstances and situation of our lives reveal it to us. To follow Christ means to claim one's own particular destiny, just as Christ claimed his own unique identity and mission. Discipleship of Jesus exemplifies the paradox of all authentic relationships—one stands alone and yet is mysteriously united with Christ.

The way of Christ is the way of love. This way of love is the yoke of life, the supportive, balancing enablement of the Spirit that empowered Jesus and, in turn, empowers us. To share that yoke of life releases the unlimited possibilities of creativity, joy, and fulfillment that are at the heart of discipleship.

"Come to me, all you that are weary and are carrying heavy burdens, and I will give you rest. Take my yoke upon you, and learn from me; for I am gentle and humble in heart, and you will find rest for your souls. For my yoke is easy, and my burden is light" (Matthew 11:28-30).

Suggested Approach to Prayer: Personal Invitation

- **Daily Prayer Pattern:**
  I quiet myself and relax in the presence of God.
  I declare my dependence on God.

- **Grace:**
  I ask to know and love Jesus more intimately so that I may follow him in faith and with courage.

- **Method:** Contemplation
  I imagine myself walking and coming upon Jesus and his disciples. He invites me to sit with them. I am attentive to the kind of day it is, whether it's sunny or overcast, warm or chilly. I am aware of the disciples and their response to my presence.

  I settle myself in quietness and listen very closely to the words of Jesus. I watch his expression as he speaks. I am aware of whether he is firm or gentle, consoling or demanding. I allow his words to resonate deeply within me. I am keenly aware of the response his words precipitate within me.

  When Jesus finishes speaking and the disciples leave, I imagine myself remaining behind. Jesus approaches me and speaks his invitation to discipleship directly to me. I share with him my feelings about saying yes to becoming his disciple—for example, excitement, fear, confusion, urgency, or anticipation.

- **Closing:**
  I speak my heart's desires to Jesus. I listen to his words to me.
  I pray the Our Father.

- **Review of Prayer:**
  In my journal I record the feelings and responses that have surfaced during my prayer.

Week One, Day 2 | Inexpressible Joy

Luke 9:28-36

Now about eight days after these sayings Jesus took with him Peter and John and James, and went up on the mountain to pray. And while he was praying, the appearance of his face changed, and his clothes became dazzling white. Suddenly they saw two men, Moses and Elijah, talking to him. They appeared in glory and were speaking of his departure, which he was about to accomplish at Jerusalem. Now Peter and his companions were weighed down with sleep; but since they had stayed awake, they saw his glory and the two men who stood with him. Just as they were leaving him, Peter said to Jesus, "Master, it is good for us to be here; let us make three dwellings, one for you, one for Moses, and one for Elijah"—not knowing what he said. While he was saying this, a cloud came and overshadowed them; and they were terrified as they entered the cloud. Then from the cloud came a voice that said, "This is my Son, my Chosen; listen to him!" When the voice had spoken, Jesus was found alone. And they kept silent and in those days told no one any of the things they had seen.

Commentary

In each of our lives there are heightened moments of joy and awareness that forever elude adequate expression. Attempts to share these experiences fall short. Our words seem flat and empty, unable to hold the transcendent fullness of the event. We search in vain for images, for symbols that can effectively convey our enthusiasm and insight.

Peter was overcome with awe in the presence of the glory of God shining forth in Jesus, his friend and leader. In his great joy, he impulsively cried out, "Let us make three dwellings!"

Instinctively Peter drew upon one of the greatest expressions of joy his people experienced, the annual communal celebration of the Feast of Tents, the Feast of Tabernacles. Each year, the Jewish people looked forward to this weeklong festival. After the autumn harvest they came in one great pilgrimage to the sanctuary to offer praise and thanksgiving for God's abundant goodness to them and to ask the Lord to send rains for the coming year. To accommodate the many people, small tents or booths—"dwellings"—were constructed wherever there was space—on hillsides and housetops, and in the corners of courtyards. The booths were made of palm branches and decorated with fruit.

The Jewish people knew how to celebrate! Magnificent processions began early in the morning, with each participant carrying a palm branch and singing songs of praise. Throughout the night, men danced in the sanctuary courtyard, dressed in white garments and carrying lighted torches. The memories of the splendor of this great feast sustained and nurtured the Jewish people throughout the entire year.

In using the symbolism associated with the Feast of Tents, Luke conveys something of the mystery of God's presence made visible in the transfigured Jesus. Peter's notion to build three booths—one for Jesus, one for Moses, and one for Elijah—gave voice to the deeper reality of his desire to prolong, to celebrate, and to mark the great moment of Jesus' transfiguration. What *did* Peter and his companions hear on the mountain that day? What *did* they see?

They saw Moses and Elijah converse with Jesus about the necessity of Jesus' own exodus, that is, his imminent suffering, death, and glorification. They saw the prophets of the Jewish Scriptures depart and give way to the new hope held in following Jesus. The disciples were privileged to receive a sustaining glimpse of the glory of Jesus' resurrection.

Peter, James, and John heard again the words spoken at Jesus' baptism, "This is my Son, my Chosen." The voice definitively confirmed the identity of Jesus as God's Son and as God's divinely elected suffering servant (Isaiah 42:1). Then, enveloped by the awesome cloud of God's presence, the disciples received the instruction, "Listen to him!"

Later, in the absence of Jesus' physical presence, the disciples, committed by faith, would discover meaning for their lives and direction for their mission through a dedicated adherence to, and dependence on, the gospel word.

"When the voice had spoken, Jesus was found alone" (Luke 9:36).

The mountain of transfiguration leads to the mount of Calvary. On the mount of transfiguration Jesus "set his face" to take the road to Jerusalem, city of his destiny (Luke 9:51). Confirmed in faith, the disciples would follow.

Like Peter, James, and John, we too join our voices with those of ancient Israel, who on the Feast of Tabernacles sang their praise and gratitude to God.

> This is the day that the LORD has made;
> let us rejoice and be glad in it. . . .
> O give thanks to the LORD, for he is good,
> for his steadfast love endures forever.
> —Psalm 118:24, 29

Suggested Approach to Prayer: The Enveloping Cloud

• Daily Prayer Pattern:
  I quiet myself and relax in the presence of God.
  I declare my dependence on God.

- **Grace:**

I ask to know and love Jesus more intimately so that I may follow him in faith and with courage.

- **Method:** Contemplation

I imagine myself being invited by Jesus to accompany him with Peter, James, and John to the mountain. As I climb, I consider in detail the arduous task I am undertaking, pausing frequently to observe the changing perspective of the terrain below. As we reach the summit, I am aware of Jesus and the disciples as they quiet themselves in prayer. I relax and enter into prayer along with them.

I contemplate Jesus in prayer as he enters deeply into communion with God. I see this union of love reflected in his face, his posture, in his total demeanor. I allow myself to absorb this glory of God in Jesus.

I become aware of the presence of Moses and Elijah and listen carefully to their conversation with Jesus. As the event unfolds, I am drawn into Peter's excitement and desire to remain here.

I become aware of the cloud of God's presence enveloping us all. I listen and am aware of my own feeling response as I hear addressed to me the words, "This is my Son, my Chosen; listen to him!"

- **Closing:**

Alone with Jesus, I let my heart express my gratitude.
I pray the Our Father.

- **Review of Prayer:**

I record in my journal the thoughts and feelings that have surfaced during my prayer.

Week One, Day 3 | Awakening

John 11:1-44

Now a certain man was ill, Lazarus of Bethany, the village of Mary and her sister Martha. Mary was the one who anointed the Lord with perfume and wiped his feet with her hair; her brother Lazarus was ill. So the sisters sent a message to Jesus, "Lord, he whom you love is ill." But when Jesus heard it, he said, "This illness does not lead to death; rather it is for God's glory, so that the Son of God may be glorified through it."

Accordingly, though Jesus loved Martha and her sister and Lazarus, after having heard that Lazarus was ill, he stayed two days longer in the place where he was. Then after this he said to the disciples, "Let us go to Judea again." The disciples said to him, "Rabbi, the Jews were just now trying to stone you, and are you going there again?" Jesus answered, "Are there not twelve hours of daylight? Those who walk during the day do not stumble, because they see the light of this world. But those who walk at night stumble, because the light is not in them." After saying this, he told them, "Our friend Lazarus has fallen asleep, but I am going there to awaken him." The disciples said to him, "Lord, if he has fallen asleep, he will be all right." Jesus, however, had been speaking about his death, but they thought that he was referring merely to sleep. Then Jesus told them plainly, "Lazarus is dead. For your sake I am glad I was not there, so that you may believe. But let us go to him." Thomas, who was called the Twin, said to his fellow disciples, "Let us also go, that we may die with him." When Jesus arrived, he found that Lazarus had already been in the tomb four days. Now Bethany was near Jerusalem, some two miles away, and many of the Jews had come to Martha and Mary to console them about their brother. When Martha heard that Jesus was coming, she went and met him, while Mary stayed at home. Martha said to Jesus, "Lord, if you had been here, my brother would not have died. But even now I know that God will give you whatever you ask of him." Jesus said to her, "Your brother will rise again." Martha said to him, "I know that he will rise again in the resurrection on the last day." Jesus said to her, "I am the resurrection and the life. Those who believe in me, even though they die, will live, and everyone who lives and believes in me will never die. Do you believe this?" She said to him, "Yes, Lord, I believe that you are the Messiah, the Son of God, the one coming into the world."

When she had said this, she went back and called her sister Mary, and told her privately, "The Teacher is here and is calling for you." And when she heard it, she got up quickly and went to him. Now Jesus had not yet come to the village, but was still at the place where Martha had met him. The Jews who were with her in the house, consoling her, saw Mary get up quickly and go out. They followed her because they thought that she was going to the tomb to weep there. When Mary came where Jesus was and saw him, she knelt at his feet and said to him, "Lord, if you had been here, my brother would not have died." When Jesus saw her weeping, and the Jews who came with her also weeping, he was greatly disturbed in spirit and deeply moved. He said, "Where have you laid him?" They said to him, "Lord, come and see." Jesus began to weep. So the Jews said, "See how he loved him!" But some of them said, "Could not he who opened the eyes of the blind man have kept this man from dying?"

Then Jesus, again greatly disturbed, came to the tomb. It was a cave, and a stone was lying against it. Jesus said, "Take away the stone." Martha, the sister of the dead man, said to him, "Lord, already there is a stench because he has been dead four days." Jesus said to her, "Did I not tell you that if you believed, you would see the glory of God?" So they took away the stone. And Jesus looked upward and said, "Father, I thank you for having heard me. I knew that you always hear me, but I have said this for the sake of the crowd standing here, so that they may believe that you sent me." When he had said this, he cried with a loud voice, "Lazarus, come out!" The dead man came out, his hands and feet bound with strips of cloth, and his face wrapped in a cloth. Jesus said to them, "Unbind him, and let him go."

Commentary

Lazarus haunts us! In him we see our own story. Like Lazarus we sleep, entombed in lethargy, loneliness, self-centeredness, and fear. We are asleep! This is *our* "tragedy."

In his play *Lazarus Laughed*, Eugene O'Neill ingeniously portrays the inescapable struggle to affirm life within death, creation within chaos (Genesis 1:2). "That is your tragedy! You forget! You forget God in you!" (58, act 1, scene 2, 189).

The sleep into which we escape is the sleep from life. It is, essentially, a denial of life. Isolation, withdrawal, and unbelief serve as the harbingers of this winter season of meaninglessness.

We allow inertia to imprison us, and rather than trust ourselves to the risks and joys of life, we choose the deceptive comfort of "sleep." In so doing, we precipitate our own catatonic death. "You wish to forget! Remembrance would imply the high duty to live as the son of God—generously!—with love!—with pride!—with laughter!" (58, act 1, scene 2, 189).

Jesus is the link from death to life. Just as clearly as he called to his friend, "Lazarus, come out!" he calls us: "Come out!" We hear his voice whenever we are attentive. It reaches deep within our entombment. We need not wait for physical death. Belief in Jesus, obedience to his words, is our passage, *now*, into eternal life.

The story of Lazarus shows us that Jesus is the one who raises life out of death. Neither belief in Jesus as the "miracle worker" nor belief in the resurrection is the key that opens the way to life. Rather, it is belief in Jesus, himself, as God's Son (62, p. 171).

The fullness of being, already present within, awaits only our yes to the person of Jesus. To be awakened from the sleep of self is to be plunged into an acute awareness of life, into all its paradoxes of suffering and hope. It allows no escape from the harsh reality of an ailing world intent on death. "It is a world dead to . . . joy. . . . Its will is so sick that it must kill in order to be aware of life at all" (58, act 3, scene 1, 330).

It is into this world of rejection and unbelief that Jesus came. In giving life to Lazarus, Jesus was setting the stage for his own death, resurrection, and glorification. Jesus had no escape, and there will be none for us: the way to life is the way of Jesus. That way is the paradoxical path of self-giving; it is laying down one's life for others (John 12:24-25; 15:13).

Jesus is the resounding yes of the Father. In Jesus the future is made present, and the end is now. The awakening of Lazarus is the promise and joy of new life for us. And Lazarus laughed! "I heard the heart of Jesus laughing in my heart. . . . And my heart reborn to love of life cried, Yes! And I laughed in the laughter of God!" (58, act 1, scene 1, 279).

Suggested Approach to Prayer: "Come Out"

• **Daily Prayer Pattern:**
I quiet myself and relax in the presence of God.
I declare my dependence on God.

• **Grace:**
I ask to know and love Jesus more intimately so that I may follow him in faith and with courage.

• **Method:** Contemplation
I imagine myself like Lazarus, entombed. I allow myself to experience the darkness, the damp chill, the aloneness, the confinement. I become aware of the walls of my tomb.

I consider prayerfully what it is in me that has given shape to the stones that form my prison. I ask myself if the stones are those of apathy, self-centeredness, fear, distrust, self-doubt, culpable ignorance, unhealed memories. . . .

I particularize my tomb by writing on each of the stones the name that gives it form. I focus my attention on the large entrance stone blocking my freedom.

In my aloneness I listen expectantly for the voice of Jesus calling me to "come out." I hear him address me by name. "_____, come out." I use these words as a repeated prayer (see p. 15), hearing them over and over, resounding in my heart. I allow these words of Jesus to penetrate the large stone and to call me forth into freedom of life with him. I allow him to unbind and free me.

• **Closing:**
I ask Mary to intercede for me that I would receive the gift of total dependence on God. I ask that I would be so detached from all things

that I would put all my talents, possessions, and achievements at the service of Christ. I pray to follow in the pattern of Christ's life—even to the end. Providing it would not be sinful on anyone's part, I pray that if it is God's wish for me, I would have, like Christ, the courage and strength to endure poverty and/or personal humiliation.

I pray the Hail Mary.

In the company of Mary, I approach Jesus and offer the same prayer, that he would obtain these graces for me from my Creator. I say the prayer Soul of Christ, on p. 164.

In the presence of Jesus and Mary, and offered by them, I approach God, my Creator. Again I make the same request.

I pray the Our Father.

• **Review of Prayer:**

I write in my journal what has surfaced in my prayer, attending especially to the feelings I experienced.

Week One, Day 4 | More Than He Knew

John 11:45-54

Many of the Jews therefore, who had come with Mary and had seen what Jesus did, believed in him. But some of them went to the Pharisees and told them what he had done. So the chief priests and the Pharisees called a meeting of the council, and said, "What are we to do? This man is performing many signs. If we let him go on like this, everyone will believe in him, and the Romans will come and destroy both our holy place and our nation." But one of them, Caiaphas, who was high priest that year, said to them, "You know nothing at all! You do not understand that it is better for you to have one man die for the people than to have the whole nation destroyed." He did not say this on his own, but being high priest that year he prophesied that Jesus was about to die for the nation, and not for the nation only, but to gather into one the dispersed children of God. So from that day on they planned to put him to death.

Jesus therefore no longer walked about openly among the Jews, but went from there to a town called Ephraim in the region near the wilderness; and he remained there with the disciples.

Commentary

He didn't know what he was saying! "It is better for you to have one man die for the people than to have the whole nation destroyed." Ironically, the words that articulated and set into motion the final liberating act of Jesus came from the lips of the leader of the opposition, Caiaphas.

High priest in that crucial year, Caiaphas spoke out of political expediency. He was under strong pressure to subdue Jesus. Fearing the destruction of the Temple by the Romans, he failed to perceive that he himself was contributing to its collapse. He was unable to make the leap of faith that would have allowed him to see Jesus as the new temple (John 2:19). Unfortunately, there were those among his followers who joined him in rejecting Jesus.

Unaware of the profound ramifications of his words, Caiaphas paradoxically effected the fulfillment of Jesus' mission. The early Christian community remembered the episode of this preliminary trial of Jesus as the unconscious prophecy of the high priest, Caiaphas.

In less than six months, Jesus had given the people two major signs of God's love. He gave sight to the man born blind (John 9); and he raised Lazarus from the dead (11:1-44).

Some believed; some did not believe. Because some believed, Jesus had to die. The enthusiasm Jesus aroused threatened those in authority and was the catalytic force that led to his death. The ultimate irony was that the death of Jesus gave birth to the very thing the Pharisees sought to eliminate—the creation of a new community!

Jesus died "not for the nation only, but to gather into one the dispersed children of God." God's love, made visible in Jesus' dying for all of humankind, enfolded gentile as well as Jew into the new Israel, the church. Caiaphas truly said more than he knew!

Suggested Approach to Prayer: Response to Jesus

• **Daily Prayer Pattern:**
I quiet myself and relax in the presence of God.
I declare my dependence on God.

• **Grace:**
I ask to know and love Jesus more intimately so that I may follow him
in faith and with courage.

• **Method:** Contemplation
As I recall the signs of Jesus' power, I imagine again the people whose
lives were transformed through his compassionate love: the man born
blind who was given sight, the woman cured of the hemorrhage, Lazarus
raised from the dead. . . .

I place myself in the crowd of onlookers who witnessed these signs
of power. I look at the people present to see if they are angry, doubtful,
threatened, excited, joyous. . . . I especially consider how the witnesses
respond to the person of Jesus. I note that some believe and others do
not. I am aware of my own heart's response to Jesus.

I imagine myself present at the impromptu gathering of the chief
priests and Pharisees. I listen attentively to the charges leveled at Jesus. I
hear the elders express their intention to execute Jesus. I become acutely
aware of my own feeling responses to the Pharisees' accusations and their
plot to kill Jesus.

I consider prayerfully that I am among the people for whom Jesus died.

• **Closing:**
I ask Mary to intercede for me that I would receive the gift of total
dependence on God. I ask that I would be so detached from all things
that I would put all my talents, possessions, and achievements at the ser-

vice of Christ. I pray to follow in the pattern of Christ's life—even to the end. Providing it would not be sinful on anyone's part, I pray that if it is God's wish for me, I would have, like Christ, the courage and strength to endure poverty and/or personal humiliation.

I pray the Hail Mary.

In the company of Mary, I approach Jesus and offer the same prayer, that he would obtain these graces for me from my Creator. I say the prayer Soul of Christ, on p. 164.

In the presence of Jesus and Mary, and offered by them, I approach God, my Creator. Again I make the same request.

I pray the Our Father.

• **Review of Prayer:**

I write in my journal what has surfaced in my prayer, attending especially to the feelings I experienced.

Week One, Day 5 | Anointed with Love

John 12:1-8

> *Six days before the Passover Jesus came to Bethany, the home of Lazarus, whom he had raised from the dead. There they gave a dinner for him. Martha served, and Lazarus was one of those at the table with him. Mary took a pound of costly perfume made of pure nard, anointed Jesus' feet, and wiped them with her hair. The house was filled with the fragrance of the perfume. But Judas Iscariot, one of his disciples (the one who was about to betray him), said, "Why was this perfume not sold for three hundred denarii and the money given to the poor?" (He said this not because he cared about the poor, but because he was a thief; he kept the common purse and used to steal what was put into it.) Jesus said, "Leave her alone. She bought it so that she might keep it for the day of my burial. You always have the poor with you, but you do not always have me."*

Commentary

An extraordinary thing happened when Jesus returned to Bethany. There was a moment so exquisitely beautiful that it was nearly inexpressible. It was one of those rare moments when a person is so overwhelmed with love for another that all reservations and self-consciousness fall away as if no one else were present, and love overflows in a fullness of expression. The moment occurred when, with precious and costly ointment, Mary anointed the feet of Jesus.

Mary responded simply and spontaneously from her deep love for Jesus. Her instinctive action revealed her subconscious love-knowledge of Jesus. Yet at the same time, by pouring oil over Jesus' feet, Mary also helped to reveal Jesus' destiny.

In anointing Jesus' feet, Mary did something that was culturally inappropriate; feet were anointed only as part of the embalming ritual. Thus, her expression of love can be understood as a prophecy of Jesus' imminent death. Even Jesus acknowledged the deeper meaning of Mary's use of the precious ointment: "She bought it so that she might keep it for the day of my burial."

"The house was filled with the fragrance of the perfume." Throughout the centuries, those who believe have remembered and celebrated the beauty of this moment. The scent that permeated the house has come to symbolize the essence of Jesus' glorious presence permeating the entire world. "The whole earth is full of his glory" (Isaiah 6:3).

Unfortunately, not all who witnessed the moment were open to seeing this glory. Judas was blind to it, his mind warped by the shadow of darkness. While those who believed saw a supreme expression of love, Judas saw only a rash extravagance, foolish and wasteful. The contrast between Mary, who loved, and Judas, who did not believe, is striking!

One in the crowd saw clearly the intent and full import of Mary's gesture of love. That one was Jesus. He countered Judas' disgruntled criticism with the reprimand, "Leave her alone. . . . You always have the poor with you, but you do not always have me."

Jesus was reminding Judas, as well as the others, of a rabbinic teaching: although almsgiving and other works of justice were considered essential, the works of mercy, of which burial was one example, had primacy and were seen to be more perfect.

Jesus was aware that the disciples he loved would soon be subjected to the radical poverty of the loss of his physical presence. He recalled the teaching not to emphasize the inevitability of social poverty, but to recognize the timeliness of Mary's extravagant offering of love toward him.

Through Mary's action of love we are privileged to see more clearly the power of Jesus' love and what our response of honor and worship of him can be. Her abandonment in love to Jesus, who passed through death and burial to glory, bears witness that only love is strong enough to transcend death (Song of Songs 8:6).

Within us, the spirit of Mary of Bethany is present to prompt and encourage our hearts to grasp the moment, to "live in love, as Christ loved us and gave himself up for us, a fragrant offering and sacrifice to God" (Ephesians 5:2).

Suggested Approach to Prayer: The Fragrance of Presence

• **Daily Prayer Pattern:**
   I quiet myself and relax in the presence of God.
   I declare my dependence on God.

• **Grace:**
   I ask to know and love Jesus more intimately so that I may follow him in faith and with courage.

• **Methods:** Contemplation and Centering
   I visualize myself at the table in Bethany. I consider the joy present among the friends who gather with Jesus. I am also aware of undercurrents of sadness and a feeling of dread.

   I look at each face around the table. I take note of what I see and feel. I watch Mary. I become aware of what her face reveals of her inner spirit as she strokes the feet of Jesus with perfumed ointment. I allow the fragrance to gently enfold me.

I imagine the fragrance as the presence of Jesus. Slowly and deeply, I breathe in Jesus' presence. I allow his presence to permeate my entire being so that every cell of my body is filled with his essence.

Within the recesses of myself, I periodically repeat the prayer, "Glory and honor to you, Lord Jesus Christ." I contemplate the face of Jesus. I see, behind his eyes, knowledge of the deeper meaning of this moment. I am *with* him. Can I find it in my heart to kneel at the feet of Jesus and, with Mary, to anoint his feet?

- **Closing:**
  I allow my heart to speak intimately and deeply to the heart of Christ. I pray the Our Father.

- **Review of Prayer:**
  In my journal, I record the thoughts and feelings that have surfaced during my time of prayer.

Week One, Day 6 | Repetition

Suggested Approach to Prayer

• **Daily Prayer Pattern:**
I quiet myself and relax in the presence of God.
I declare my dependence on God.

• **Grace:**
I ask God to allow me to enter into sorrow as I stay with Christ in his sufferings, borne on my behalf and because of my sins.

• **Method:** Repetition
In preparation, I review my prayer periods by reading my journal of the past week. I select for my repetition the period of prayer in which I was most deeply moved, or one in which I experienced a lack of emotional response, or one in which I was grasped with insight, or one in which I experienced confusion. I use the method with which I approached the passage initially. I open myself to hear again God's word to me in that particular passage.

• **Review of Prayer:**
I write in my journal any feelings, experiences, or insights that have surfaced in this "second listening."

If Anyone Wants to Be a Follower of Mine

Week Two, Day 1 | He Who Comes

Matthew 21:1-17

When they had come near Jerusalem and had reached Bethphage, at the Mount of Olives, Jesus sent two disciples, saying to them, "Go into the village ahead of you, and immediately you will find a donkey tied, and a colt with her; untie them and bring them to me. If anyone says anything to you, just say this, 'The Lord needs them.' And he will send them immediately." This took place to fulfill what had been spoken through the prophet, saying,

"Tell the daughter of Zion,
Look, your king is coming to you,
humble, and mounted on a donkey,
and on a colt, the foal of a donkey."

The disciples went and did as Jesus had directed them; they brought the donkey and the colt, and put their cloaks on them, and he sat on them. A very large crowd spread their cloaks on the road, and others cut branches from the trees and spread them on the road. The crowds that went ahead of him and that followed were shouting,

"Hosanna to the Son of David!
Blessed is the one who comes in the name of the Lord!
Hosanna in the highest heaven!"

When he entered Jerusalem, the whole city was in turmoil, asking, "Who is this?" The crowds were saying, "This is the prophet Jesus from Nazareth in Galilee."

Then Jesus entered the temple and drove out all who were selling and buying in the temple, and he overturned the tables of the

*money changers and the seats of those who sold doves. He said
to them, "It is written,*

> *'My house shall be called a house of prayer';*
>   *but you are making it a den of robbers."*

*The blind and the lame came to him in the temple, and he cured
them. But when the chief priests and the scribes saw the amazing things that he did, and heard the children crying out in the
temple, "Hosanna to the Son of David," they became angry and
said to him, "Do you hear what these are saying?" Jesus said to
them, "Yes; have you never read,*

> *'Out of the mouths of infants and nursing babies*
>   *you have prepared praise for yourself'?"*

*He left them, went out of the city to Bethany, and spent the night
there.*

Commentary

What would become of us if we did not hope, if we did not nurture hope,
if we did not risk believing in the unexpected and the unseen?

Jesus Christ *is* our hope (1 Timothy 1:1). On the occasion of his dramatic
entry into the city of Jerusalem, Jesus was seen and celebrated as the fulfillment of the hope that had shaped centuries of longing and expectation.

His entry was a highly charged symbolic drama. Jesus, himself, set the
stage. It was he who chose to make his ascent into the city from the Mount
of Olives, a place long identified with messianic hope (Zechariah 14:4). By
deliberately choosing to enter the city riding on a donkey, long associated
with kings in peaceful times, Jesus presented himself as a king of peace.

All the aspects of his entrance into Jerusalem revealed Jesus' radical claim to be the Son of David, the hoped-for Messiah. An unmistakable note of majesty and kingship accompanied Jesus' progress through the city toward the Temple, where he would assert his liberating authority as God's Son.

The people were exuberant in response, spreading cloaks and branches in his path. Indeed, they welcomed him royally, shouting, "Hosanna!" The sight of Jesus and the significance of the event so exhilarated the people that the entire city of Jerusalem seemed shaken to its very foundation.

Jesus accepted their recognition and homage. For the first time, on the threshold of his passion, he allowed the people to claim him as their Messiah. Once again, he had extended himself in love, offering to them a challenging invitation to open their hearts to him. They recognized, accepted, and heralded him as the one "who comes in the name of the Lord."

Jesus came humbly, a coming that contrasted sharply with the messianic expectations of the time. His arena was not the palaces of diplomacy where political alliances were forged, nor was it the battlefield where military victory was sought at any cost. No, Jesus moved among the people, among the blind and the despairing, offering hope to all those suffering in body or in spirit. His stance was one of humility, the humility of authenticity, a humility born of inner strength.

On the day of his entrance into Jerusalem, Jesus, the people's Messiah, revealed a fearless and uncompromising strength as he proceeded directly to the center of the city, into the sanctuary, reclaiming and restoring the Temple as the house of God.

The marvelous procession into Jerusalem and the manifestation of the healing, restoring power of Jesus foreshadowed the fullness of time when Jesus would return in glory. This occasion, like that of the transfiguration, filled the early Christians with hope and sustained them in their hour of darkness.

We, as contemporary Christians, are part of the great procession of those who have followed Jesus. Filled with his Spirit, we become a sign of hope for others. In oneness with Jesus, we bring his healing presence to an anguished world, a world broken and yearning for wholeness.

Suggested Approach to Prayer: The Man on the Donkey

- **Daily Prayer Pattern:**
  I quiet myself and relax in the presence of God.
  I declare my dependence on God.

- **Grace:**
  I ask to know and love Jesus more intimately so that I may follow him in faith and with courage.

- **Method:** Contemplation
  I visualize myself in the crowd on a narrow street in Jerusalem. I imagine in great detail the sights, sounds, and smells of the busy, overcrowded city.

  I hear the excitement of the people as the procession approaches. I am aware of the jostling of the people around me as they strain to catch a glimpse of the man on the donkey. I listen as I hear him acclaimed the Son of David, the one who "comes in the name of the Lord."

  I am aware of my feeling response as I see him approach, my excitement . . . confusion . . . fear . . . longing . . . hope . . . doubt . . . expectation. . . . I imagine what action I feel moved to take. Do I follow along, or do I withdraw? I am aware of my feelings as I enter or do not enter into the procession.

  As Jesus passes, I focus on his face and pay particular attention to his expression. I imagine what he is thinking at this moment. I hear someone shout, "Who is this?" I let my heart respond.

- **Closing:**
  I ask Mary to intercede for me that I would receive the gift of total dependence on God. I ask that I would be so detached from all things that I would put all my talents, possessions, and achievements at the ser-

vice of Christ. I pray to follow in the pattern of Christ's life—even to the end. Providing it would not be sinful on anyone's part, I pray that if it is God's wish for me, I would have, like Christ, the courage and strength to endure poverty and/or personal humiliation.

I pray the Hail Mary.

In the company of Mary, I approach Jesus and offer the same prayer, that he would obtain these graces for me from my Creator. I pray the prayer Soul of Christ, on p. 164.

In the presence of Jesus and Mary, and offered by them, I approach God, my Creator. Again I make the same request.

I pray the Our Father.

• **Review of Prayer:**

I write in my journal what has surfaced in my prayer as a call to follow Jesus more closely, attending especially to the feelings I experienced.

Week Two, Day 2 | Harvest Yield

John 12:23-32

> *Jesus answered them, "The hour has come for the Son of Man to be glorified. Very truly, I tell you, unless a grain of wheat falls into the earth and dies, it remains just a single grain; but if it dies, it bears much fruit. Those who love their life lose it, and those who hate their life in this world will keep it for eternal life. Whoever serves me must follow me, and where I am, there will my servant be also. Whoever serves me, the Father will honor.*
>
> *"Now my soul is troubled. And what should I say—'Father, save me from this hour'? No, it is for this reason that I have come to this hour. Father, glorify your name." Then a voice came from heaven, "I have glorified it, and I will glorify it again." The crowd standing there heard it and said that it was thunder. Others said, "An angel has spoken to him." Jesus answered, "This voice has come for your sake, not for mine. Now is the judgment of this world; now the ruler of this world will be driven out. And I, when I am lifted up from the earth, will draw all people to myself."*

Commentary

The "hour" of Jesus is our *present* hour. The hour is not an hour of death, but an hour of birth.

Jesus drew on the fecundity of nature to illustrate his hour and to exemplify his glorification, the harvest of life that his death would yield. The imagery of the seed yielding to harvest awakens in us the rich experience and splendor of nature's fruitfulness:

> In perpetual transformation, the humble "rotting" seed lengthens into stock and sprouting leaves, long stem grows into dense bud, whence the blossom bursts forth in all its diversity into the green and gold of leaves and thence into the radiant color of the flower, culminates into the reversal by which the scented fragility of the blossom becomes the concentrated mature fruit, again with its infinite variety of form, color, consistency, taste, and smell (55, p. 51).

Jesus is the prototype of the giving of self of those who believe. "Like a root out of dry ground. . . . he had no form or majesty . . . wounded for our transgression . . . oppressed . . . afflicted. . . . He was cut off from the land of the living" (Isaiah 53:2-3, 5, 7-8).

The Greek gentiles, to whom Jesus replied in this passage from John, are the prototype of the mature fruit that issues forth through Jesus' offering of self. "He shall see his offspring. . . . Out of his anguish he shall see light; he shall find satisfaction through his knowledge" (Isaiah 53:10-11).

The presence of the gentiles symbolizes the universality of the Christian community, which embraces all diversities in its fold. The occasion of the gentiles' coming to Jesus signaled for him the arrival of his hour. The time for reconciliation had come. All would be drawn together in him through the outpouring of himself in love.

A people newly formed through his death and resurrection announced a new era. This birthing of a community was not without labor and suffering. Jesus was fearful, and he struggled with the temptation to ask the Father to spare him. Yet trusting in God's love, he surrendered, letting go of his fear of death, of his clinging to life.

Jesus' submission is the model for our own. In bringing forth new life, he was unable to escape death. His followers, too, will be faced throughout their lives with choosing death to selfishness as the only true path to life. Therefore, love for life means "hating" one's life, that is, hating within one's life any self-seeking that serves as an obstacle to loving. "In the evening of life," said St. John of the Cross, "we will be judged by love."

The voice of the Father affirms Jesus' selfless prayer "Father, glorify your name." Once again, as in the transfiguration, God's glory became visible. God reassured Jesus, and Jesus, in turn, reassures us. His death is the culminating triumph of God's evolving plan for creation. All things created are being drawn into oneness with Jesus and carried in his spirit into eternal life, which, present even now, continues to burst forth in a "rich harvest."

Suggested Approach to Prayer: My Tree

• **Daily Prayer Pattern:**
I quiet myself and relax in the presence of God.
I declare my dependence on God.

• **Grace:**
I ask to know and love Jesus more intimately so that I may follow him more closely in faith and with courage.

• **Method:** Contemplation
I imagine myself returning to the place of my birth. I consider what the weather is like on my birth day—sunny, overcast, stormy? . . . I see the fruit tree, the seed of which I imagine was planted by my parents on the day of my birth.

I consider where my tree was planted, perhaps in the corner of the yard, in an open field, one of many in an orchard. . . . I am aware of my feelings as I see my tree for the first time in many years. For example, I might feel excitement, disappointment, or surprise as I see how tall it is, how full it is, whether it is straight or crooked. I circle around my tree, viewing it from different angles, seeing the spread of its branches, the color of its foliage. I approach it and touch the bark, and I am aware of its texture, whether it feels smooth, irregular, coarse.

I consider the fruit hanging from the branches—whether it is abundant or skimpy or barren. I take careful note of the quality of the fruit, its color, its fragrance. I pick a fruit, feel its contours, taste it. I consider how I feel about my tree, what I like or do not like about it. I speak to my tree, and I hear it respond to me. I become the tree. I consider how it feels to be my tree, to own as my own its stature, its character, and its fruit.

I see Jesus approach. I consider how he looks at me, what he says to me, whether or not he takes a fruit from my branches. He speaks to me of my fruit, and I respond. I continue to listen to and speak with Jesus. After the dialogue with Jesus, I become myself again. As I prepare to leave, I look reverently at my tree, prayerfully considering how all I am was present in the promise of its seed. I consider if and how my tree and its fruit have changed since I arrived. I become aware of how my feelings about my tree and the seeds of its fruitfulness have changed.

• **Closing:**
I ask Mary to intercede for me that I would receive the gift of total dependence on God. I ask that I would be so detached from all things that I would put all my talents, possessions, and achievements at the service of Christ. I pray to follow in the pattern of Christ's life—even to the end. Providing it would not be sinful on anyone's part, I pray that if it is God's wish for me, I would have, like Christ, the courage and strength to endure poverty and/or personal humiliation.

I pray the Hail Mary.

In the company of Mary, I approach Jesus and offer the same prayer, that he would obtain these graces for me from my Creator. I pray the prayer Soul of Christ, on p. 164.

In the presence of Jesus and Mary, and offered by them, I approach God, my Creator. Again I make the same request.

I pray the Our Father.

• **Review of Prayer:**

I write in my journal what has surfaced in my prayer, attending especially to the feelings I experienced.

Week Two, Day 3 | A Basin, Some Water, and a Towel

John 13:1-16

Now before the festival of the Passover, Jesus knew that his hour had come to depart from this world and go to the Father. Having loved his own who were in the world, he loved them to the end. The devil had already put it into the heart of Judas son of Simon Iscariot to betray him. And during supper Jesus, knowing that the Father had given all things into his hands, and that he had come from God and was going to God, got up from the table, took off his outer robe, and tied a towel around himself. Then he poured water into a basin and began to wash the disciples' feet and to wipe them with the towel that was tied around him. He came to Simon Peter, who said to him, "Lord, are you going to wash my feet?" Jesus answered, "You do not know now what I am doing, but later you will understand." Peter said to him, "You will never wash my feet." Jesus answered, "Unless I wash you, you have no share with me." Simon Peter said to him, "Lord, not my feet only but also my hands and my head!" Jesus said to him, "One who has bathed does not need to wash, except for the feet, but is entirely clean. And you are clean, though not all of you." For he knew who was to betray him; for this reason he said, "Not all of you are clean."

After he had washed their feet, had put on his robe, and had returned to the table, he said to them, "Do you know what I have done to you? You call me Teacher and Lord—and you are right, for that is what I am. So if I, your Lord and Teacher, have washed your feet, you also ought to wash one another's feet. For

I have set you an example, that you also should do as I have done to you. Very truly, I tell you, servants are not greater than their master, nor are messengers greater than the one who sent them.

Commentary

A basin, some water, and a towel—ordinary means to serve an extraordinary love!

Jesus' extravagant love for his disciples motivated his gentle and humble act of washing their feet. This deliberate action by Jesus also spoke of the profound level of awareness he had of his impending death.

Just as Mary's anointing of Jesus' feet foretold his future embalming, Jesus' washing his apostles' feet symbolized his approaching death—the ultimate act of his love—which would cleanse the apostles of their sinfulness and ensure their heritage in him.

This incident is one of the most tender in the gospels. Washing his apostles' feet was for Jesus, and for them, an intimate moment of transparent vulnerability and surrender. Not even the evil intent active within Judas could destroy its spirit of goodness.

This simple, human gesture not only gave expression to the love that had grown between Jesus and his disciples throughout the years of his public ministry, but it also represented the disciples' initiation into their own mature ministry, which would take place without their master's physical presence.

"I have set you an example, that you also should do as I have done to you."

As Jesus laid down his garments, he was deeply conscious of the nearness of the hour in which he would lay down his life for those he loved. Wrapping a towel around his waist in the manner of a slave, Jesus, the Master and Lord, voluntarily submitted himself to the radicalness of a love that serves. In this reversal of roles, Jesus called his disciples, also, to become willing servants of love, even to the point of laying down *their* lives for others (John 15:13).

The water Jesus poured over their feet was the cleansing water of purification, a symbol of his self-emptying death. So wonderful was his act of love that Peter and the others would be able to comprehend the full import of it only after Jesus' death and resurrection. Only then would they understand the baptismal symbolism of their experience. In their newly created community they would experience the joy of oneness with the risen Christ and grasp the full significance of baptism in the Spirit.

A basin, some water, and a towel had become for the apostles, and for us, a powerful prophetic symbol of the wholeness of Jesus' life, death, resurrection, and ascension—the wholeness of his love.

Suggested Approach to Prayer: Bathed in Love

• **Daily Prayer Pattern:**
  I quiet myself and relax in the presence of God.
  I declare my dependence on God.

• **Grace:**
  I ask to know and love Jesus more intimately so that I may follow him more closely in faith and with courage.

• **Method:** Contemplation
  I imagine Jesus walking into our church on a Sunday morning. I see him open his hands to us and say, in a way that speaks to our hearts, "I have not called you servants, but friends." I am aware of what passes through my mind, what surges in my heart, as I hear him say these words.

I see Jesus look over the gathered assembly. He calls forth a number of people. I hear him call the names of several others, and I see their response, how they rise reluctantly or eagerly. . . . I hear him call my name and see him look at me lovingly and humbly. I take care to experience within me both of these attitudes of Christ as he looks at me.

I see Jesus gather those he has specially called. He invites us to be seated in the sanctuary. Then, deliberately and lovingly, he brings a basin of water and some towels. He disrobes and stands before us, stripped except for a loincloth. I notice the shadow of scars on his side . . . his hands . . . his feet.

Jesus kneels before me and begins to wash my feet. I am acutely aware of my feelings, perhaps of embarrassment . . . or wonder and awe . . . tenderness. . . . When Jesus has finished, he says to me, "As I have done for you, go and do likewise for the others."

I consider, "To whom will I go? How will the intimacy and love of Jesus for me spill over into my family? Into my faith community? Into anyone I encounter?"

• **Closing:**

I conclude my prayer with a heartfelt conversation with Christ. I let it be a prayer of personal friendship, expressing my hopes, my needs; and my praise, my thanks, and my love.
I pray the Our Father.

• **Review of Prayer:**

I write in my journal the feelings and insights that have surfaced during my prayer.

Week Two, Day 4 | In Remembrance

Luke 22:14-23

When the hour came, he took his place at the table, and the apostles with him. He said to them, "I have eagerly desired to eat this Passover with you before I suffer; for I tell you, I will not eat it until it is fulfilled in the kingdom of God." Then he took a cup, and after giving thanks he said, "Take this and divide it among yourselves; for I tell you that from now on I will not drink of the fruit of the vine until the kingdom of God comes." Then he took a loaf of bread, and when he had given thanks, he broke it and gave it to them, saying, "This is my body, which is given for you. Do this in remembrance of me." And he did the same with the cup after supper, saying, "This cup that is poured out for you is the new covenant in my blood. But see, the one who betrays me is with me, and his hand is on the table. For the Son of Man is going as it has been determined, but woe to that one by whom he is betrayed!" Then they began to ask one another which one of them it could be who would do this.

Commentary

Our God is a God who remembers. In Jesus, God lives out his remembering.

On the evening before his death, Jesus shared a meal with his apostles. This last supper was a celebration of joyful remembrance, thanksgiving, and promise. Together they celebrated God's faithfulness to them throughout their history. They remembered how God had led them, had never abandoned them, had always been present.

This last meal, colored as it was by grief at Jesus' approaching death and impending betrayal, was, nevertheless, redolent with the promise Jesus made to them. Jesus promised never to leave them, but to be present to them in a new, even fuller way. This shared meal initiated the apostles into a new relationship with Jesus, a relationship of mutuality, in which they, too, had a commitment. It was to be a bond of loving friendship transcending death (Song of Songs 8:6).

The celebration took place within the context of the Passover festival, which was celebrated annually by the Jewish people. Passover recalled and relived the pivotal experience in their history when God delivered them from Egyptian slavery (Exodus 12:1-14).

It was a festival of praise and elaborate ritual. Recalling the Exodus, the rite began with a preliminary blessing and a cup of wine. Bitter herbs were then served to recall the bitterness of their suffering in Egypt. At this point in the meal the youngest male child would ask, "What does this night mean?" His father would respond by telling the story of God's faithfulness to the people of God, thereby creating for future memory the image of a loving God who remembers.

After singing psalms and drinking a second cup of wine, new unleavened bread was blessed. It was eaten with the roasted Passover lamb. The blessing and drinking of a third cup of wine brought the meal to a close. The ritual remembrance was concluded with the singing of psalms and praise: "Blessed is the one who comes in the name of the LORD" (Psalm 118:26).

In Jesus, God lives out this remembrance—this everlasting faithfulness and loving kindness. In Jesus' life, the history of God's people, Israel, is recapitulated (Psalm 136).

At the Last Supper, Jesus reinterpreted and brought to greater fullness the symbols of the paschal ritual, interpreting the symbols in terms of himself. Jesus took the first cup and proclaimed the coming of the kingdom, when he would drink wine with them again.

He identified the unleavened bread with his own body. No longer to be known as the bread of affliction eaten in bondage, this bread was to be the bread of freedom. Through this bread, the disciples would experience the liberating presence of Christ with them, individually and communally.

Jesus identified the third cup of the paschal meal with the new covenant in his blood (Jeremiah 31:31-32). The sacrifice of the Passover lamb had given way to Jesus' offering of his own self, the offering of his entire life, culminating now in his death. Because blood is life (Leviticus 17:11) and the flow of blood unites in one life, Jesus' blood symbolizes and effects a forceful union between God and the people of God. Jesus' covenant of blood is a covenant of life.

"Do this in remembrance of me." Jesus told his disciples to continue living their relationship of love with him through the continuing celebration of his presence among them. He promised that in their future remembering, in the memorializing of his presence, he would re-present himself to the Christian community whenever they, recalling his last shared meal with them, blessed and shared bread and wine.

In this living re-presentation of himself in love for them, they would experience their union with him and with each other. Through their active participation in this memorial celebration, they would be incorporated in the power of Jesus' death and resurrection, and their lives, like his, would be blessed and given for others.

"Do this in remembrance of me." In bread broken and wine poured, we receive our lives, the healing of what has been, the joy of who we truly are, the promise of all we may yet be.

Suggested Approach to Prayer: At the Table

- **Daily Prayer Pattern:**
  I quiet myself and relax in the presence of God.
  I declare my dependence on God.

- **Grace:**
  I ask to know and love Jesus more intimately and that I may enter into sorrow as I stay with Christ in his suffering.

- **Method:** Contemplation
  I imagine myself at the table with Jesus and his apostles. I see the room in which all are gathered and notice whether it is large or small, well lit or dark, warm or chilly. . . . I see the table, its cloth, the cups and other dishes. . . .

  I observe the disciples as they recline at table, allowing myself time to take note of each individual's expression—whether he appears to be joyous, fearful, expectant, sad. . . . I listen attentively to their words, particularly to the way the words are spoken—whether they connote love, kindness, grief, fear, deceit. . . .

  Aware of Jesus' approaching death, I focus my attention on him. I see his expression, the way he looks at his disciples. I allow myself to contemplate his face. I am particularly aware of the feelings I experience when I look into his face.

  I hear Jesus speak. I listen as he leads his followers through the Passover ritual. I watch and listen as he blesses and shares bread and wine with them, and as he invites them to do this in memory of him. I am attentive to how I feel—for example, awed, confused, blessed; included or left out. . . .

  I ask Jesus, "What does this night mean?" I allow myself to be quietly present as I receive Jesus' response within me.

- **Closing:**

I ask Mary to intercede for me that I would receive the gift of total dependence on God. I ask that I may be so detached from all things that I put all my talents, possessions, and achievements at the service of Christ.

I pray to follow in the pattern of Christ's life—even to the end. Providing it would not be sinful on anyone's part, I pray that if it is God's wish for me, I would have, like Christ, the courage and strength to endure poverty and/or personal humiliation.

I pray the Hail Mary.

In the company of Mary, I approach Jesus and offer the same prayer, that he would obtain these graces for me from my Creator. I pray the prayer Soul of Christ, on p. 164.

In the presence of Jesus and Mary, and offered by them, I approach God, my Creator. Again I make the same request.

I pray the Our Father.

- **Review of Prayer:**

I write in my journal what has surfaced in my prayer as a call to follow Jesus more closely, attending especially to the feelings I experienced.

Week Two, Day 5 | The Secret Place, the Sacred Place

John 17:1-26

After Jesus had spoken these words, he looked up to heaven and said, "Father, the hour has come; glorify your Son so that the Son may glorify you, since you have given him authority over all people, to give eternal life to all whom you have given him. And this is eternal life, that they may know you, the only true God, and Jesus Christ whom you have sent. I glorified you on earth by finishing the work that you gave me to do. So now, Father, glorify me in your own presence with the glory that I had in your presence before the world existed.

"I have made your name known to those whom you gave me from the world. They were yours, and you gave them to me, and they have kept your word. Now they know that everything you have given me is from you; for the words that you gave to me I have given to them, and they have received them and know in truth that I came from you; and they have believed that you sent me. I am asking on their behalf; I am not asking on behalf of the world, but on behalf of those whom you gave me, because they are yours. All mine are yours, and yours are mine; and I have been glorified in them. And now I am no longer in the world, but they are in the world, and I am coming to you. Holy Father, protect them in your name that you have given me, so that they may be one, as we are one. While I was with them, I protected them in your name that you have given me. I guarded them, and not one of them was lost except the one destined to be lost, so that the scripture might be fulfilled. But now I am coming to you,

and I speak these things in the world so that they may have my joy made complete in themselves. I have given them your word, and the world has hated them because they do not belong to the world, just as I do not belong to the world. I am not asking you to take them out of the world, but I ask you to protect them from the evil one. They do not belong to the world, just as I do not belong to the world. Sanctify them in the truth; your word is truth. As you have sent me into the world, so I have sent them into the world. And for their sakes I sanctify myself, so that they also may be sanctified in truth.

"I ask not only on behalf of these, but also on behalf of those who will believe in me through their word, that they may all be one. As you, Father, are in me and I am in you, may they also be in us, so that the world may believe that you have sent me. The glory that you have given me I have given them, so that they may be one, as we are one, I in them and you in me, that they may become completely one, so that the world may know that you have sent me and have loved them even as you have loved me. Father, I desire that those also, whom you have given me, may be with me where I am, to see my glory, which you have given me because you loved me before the foundation of the world.

"Righteous Father, the world does not know you, but I know you; and these know that you have sent me. I made your name known to them, and I will make it known, so that the love with which you have loved me may be in them, and I in them."

"Father, the hour has come:
glorify your son
so that your son may glorify you."

Abba, loving and gracious God,
    You have been with me always.
    You are with me now as I am about to die.

        Hear my prayer;
        Remember your promise.

I pray
    that your goodness will be revealed
        in my life
            and
            in my dying.

        Remember your promise, O God.

I pray
    not for myself
I pray
    for all those I love.
I pray
    that my death will be for them
        a new beginning . . .
            a beginning
                of seeing and knowing you,
        an entry
            into love with you,
            a love unique . . .

"I pray for them."

Abba, near and compassionate God,

  As I am about to leave them,
  I hold in my heart those I most love.

  I have planted your name in their hearts.
      Your word dwells there.

          Be with them.
          Comfort them.
          Protect them.

      Lead them into healing.
      Guide them in truth.

Gift them, Lord God, with the joy of being in your presence.

"May they all be one."

Abba, God of the future, God of hope.

  I place before you all of creation—
      those born
          and
      those to be born.

I celebrate
    dreams not yet dreamed,
    hopes expected, yet unseen.

I am filled with utter confidence—
    I trust in your promise.
    You have given me
      a glimpse of yourself
      shining
      in the love

                of those who believe
                of those who have found

the secret place   the sacred space

                of
             oneness
                in
              YOU

Suggested Approach to Prayer: The Mind and Heart of Jesus

- **Daily Prayer Pattern:**
  I quiet myself and relax in the presence of God.
  I declare my dependence on God.

- **Grace:**
  I ask to know and love Jesus more intimately so that I share in his thoughts and feelings as he enters into his passion.

- **Method:** Meditative Reading
  I imagine Jesus at prayer. I enter into the mind and heart of Jesus on the night before he died. I allow myself to experience his love and his concern, his prayer for those he loved.

  I slowly read John 17:1-26. I pause periodically to allow the words and phrases to resonate within the realm of my own experience. I respond to Christ and his love for me. I am aware of my feeling response, that of gratitude, awe, amazement. . . .

- **Closing:**
  I let my heart speak to Christ.
  I close with an Our Father.

- **Review of Prayer:**
  In my journal, I record my own prayer response to Jesus' prayer.

Week Two, Day 6 | Repetition

Suggested Approach to Prayer

- **Daily Prayer Pattern:**
  I quiet myself and relax in the presence of God.
  I declare my dependence on God.

- **Grace:**
  I ask God to allow me to enter into sorrow as I stay with Christ in his suffering, borne on my behalf and because of my sins.

- **Method:** Repetition
  In preparation, I review my prayer periods since the last repetition day. I select for my repetition the period of prayer in which I was most deeply moved, or the one in which I experienced a lack of emotional response, or one in which I was grasped with insight or experienced confusion. I use the method with which I approached the passage initially.
  I open myself to hear again God's word to me in that particular passage.

- **Review of Prayer:**
  I write in my journal any feelings, experiences, or insights that have surfaced in this "second listening."

The Soldiers Twisted Some Thorns into a Crown

Week Three, Day 1 | Out of the Darkness

Mark 14:32-42

> *They went to a place called Gethsemane; and he said to his disciples, "Sit here while I pray." He took with him Peter and James and John, and began to be distressed and agitated. And he said to them, "I am deeply grieved, even to death; remain here, and keep awake." And going a little farther, he threw himself on the ground and prayed that, if it were possible, the hour might pass from him. He said, "Abba, Father, for you all things are possible; remove this cup from me; yet, not what I want, but what you want." He came and found them sleeping; and he said to Peter, "Simon, are you asleep? Could you not keep awake one hour? Keep awake and pray that you may not come into the time of trial; the spirit indeed is willing, but the flesh is weak." And again he went away and prayed, saying the same words. And once more he came and found them sleeping, for their eyes were very heavy; and they did not know what to say to him. He came a third time and said to them, "Are you still sleeping and taking your rest? Enough! The hour has come; the Son of Man is betrayed into the hands of sinners. Get up, let us be going. See, my betrayer is at hand."*

Your presence, Father . . . I approach.
I have very little time, as you well know.
Do you recognize my voice?
Must I reintroduce myself? . . .
You surely remember, Father? . . .

Always you have heard *my* voice,
Always you have saluted me
with a rainbow, a raven, a plague, something.
But now I see nothing. This time
you show me
Nothing at all . . .

                    (12, part 2)

Commentary

This anguished prayer might have been Jesus' own as he entered into his
agony. Through the use of the *kaddish*, the profound Jewish prayer for the
dead, Leonard Bernstein has given poetic, as well as musical, expression to
the universal human experience of suffering and surrender. His composition
touches a chord of resonance in every human heart.

Can Jesus, whose entire life had been an experience of God's loving presence, now, in the garden of Gethsemane, be crying out for mere recognition?
Can Jesus, whose life, whose every word and action mirrored his intimate
union with God, possibly be experiencing such *godforsakenness?*

The horror and the pain, the confusion, the alienation, and the deadly anxiety that Jesus experienced in the garden is nearly indescribable. The abyss of
human aloneness and fear has always eluded adequate expression, yet ironically this very experience of intimate and intense suffering serves as the caul-
dron of heroism and creativity. One can only imagine the sincerity and love
with which Mark sought to convey the suffering of Jesus.

The struggle throughout the ages to give expression to the profoundly
human experience of self-acceptance and surrender has shaped and inspired
generations.

The prayer that is forming in the heart of Christ as he descends from the upper room and passes through the city gate to the garden is the prayer of one who is being thrust down into nothingness. In the bleakness of this void, Jesus must grapple with the ultimate meaning of life.

In facing death, Jesus encounters the finality of life's distortion—sin, the alienation from God. His boundless love for humankind and solidarity with all creation makes Jesus totally open and vulnerable, and this very openness of loving exposes him to the crushing weight of sin (Isaiah 53:10). Only Jesus, who experiences the ultimate nearness to God, can fully grasp the absurd tragedy and horror of sin. So great is his awareness of the world's loss that, overwhelmed by love, he literally experiences the loneliness and forsakenness of his loss (53:4). Crushed and powerless, almost despairing, Jesus cries out into the dark void one word, "Abba."

He who came from heaven presses himself into the sin-scarred earth, seeking protection in a hole where only death is master (64, p. 223).

"Abba"—the primal cry resounding against the impenetrable darkness of sin. "Abba"—the unanswerable plea for mercy and relief. "Abba"—the last desperate cry that precedes the capitulation of total weakness, making way for God's grace of surrender.

The surrender of Jesus to God stands in sharp contrast to the response of the apostles. He dares to enter the darkness; they sleep through the night. Yet, his acceptance reconciles their denials (Isaiah 53:11).

Through Jesus' total surrender, God's plan for Jesus is brought to fulfillment. The absolute emptiness of Jesus invites the absolute gift of God's grace. Nothing changes. Jesus will be "handed over" to death. Everything changes! Filled with God's strength, Jesus rises to face this betrayer: "Get up, let us be going."

Suggested Approach to Prayer: Into the Garden

• **Daily Prayer Pattern:**
  I quiet myself and relax in the presence of God.
  I declare my dependence on God.

• **Grace:**
  I ask to share in Christ's agony, to feel sorrow with Christ in sorrow, to
be anguished with Christ's anguish, even to experience tears because of
Christ's love for me.

• **Method:** Contemplation
  In the company of Jesus, I leave the room of the supper. Slowly I
descend the steps and walk through the city. I walk beside Jesus as he
makes his entry through the gate into the garden. In great detail, I imagine the physical surroundings that are part of our short journey: how
dark it has become, the temperature of the night air, the winding path,
the presence of the trees, the sounds and scents of the night.

  I take particular note of Jesus, of his facial expression and posture, and
what they reveal of his inner attitude. I see Jesus as he withdraws into a
private space of prayer. As I contemplate his deepening anguish, I ponder
the depth of love that moves one to such profound sorrow.

  I consider what it would be like and how I would respond if someone
I loved were to be condemned for a serious crime—perhaps a friend . . .
my spouse . . . my child. . . . I consider how their suffering, their shame
and despair, their utter isolation would be my own. I consider how over-
whelmingly poignant my pain would be, how helpless I would feel, how
desperate would be my prayer. . . .

  Having considered my own vulnerability in loving, I move to consider the depth of pain Jesus must have endured as he dared to embrace the entire world in unlimited love, as he suffered the sinfulness, the condemnation, and the alienation of those he loved.

- **Closing:**

I speak with Jesus, sharing with him how my own human experience of loving gives me a glimpse into his deep compassion. I speak to him of my deep gratitude for his loving me, my loved ones, and the entire world with such a total self-giving love. I join with Jesus in offering his prayer of surrender, "Abba, not my will but yours be done."

I pray the Our Father.

- **Review of Prayer:**

I record in my journal the feelings and insights that have surfaced during my time of prayer.

Week Three, Day 2 | Abba—Our Father

Matthew 6:9-13

> *Pray then in this way:*
> *Our Father in heaven,*
> *hallowed be your name.*
> *Your kingdom come.*
> *Your will be done,*
> *on earth as it is in heaven.*
> *Give us this day our daily bread.*
> *And forgive us our debts,*
> *as we also have forgiven our debtors.*
> *And do not bring us to the time of trial,*
> *but rescue us from the evil one.*

Our Father
　In the garden
　　dark compost of human hunger
　　chaotic womb of possibility
Births—in lightening and love—surrender!
　One moment, one time
　　transparent grail
　　　of all time
　　　　every moment.

Earth arching to meet her maker
Energy leaping from pole to pole
   and all
      emerging
      converging
The Stillpoint, Son of Man and Son of God
   prays
     "Our Father."

Commentary

The Lord's Prayer reflects the spirit in which Jesus lived his entire life. It is as if every daily moment of commitment, every hour of contemplation, every spontaneous turning to God somehow shaped this profound prayer of praise and petition. Not surprising, in the time of his greatest testing, in the garden of Gethsemane, the words that rose from Jesus' heart echoed those of the Our Father.

By addressing God as "our Father," Jesus not only claimed his identity as God's Son, he also acknowledged his solidarity with all women and men for all time. Because of Jesus and his love for us, we too can pray, "*our* Father" (Romans 8:14-15).

The prayer has a sense of urgency, a "here, now, and soon" (20, p. 198); unfortunately, frequent and thoughtless repetition has dissipated some of its immediacy. Too many Christians have lost a sense of expectation for the second coming, the Parousia.

"Your kingdom come." The expected and hoped-for kingdom is a time and a place, a here and a now, present yet always evolving. It is a movement forward in trust that magnetically charges and draws all human hearts.

Jesus prayed that this kingdom of love would be actualized in earthly history. He prayed that the name of God—Father, Mother, Creator—would be cherished and thereby authentically shape the lives of his followers as sons and daughters of God.

Jesus' prayer that God's "will be done" urges us to enter into collaboration with God, to make a personal commitment of total dedication to do all we can, within our own situation and circumstances, to bring the goodness of God to full realization. Like Jesus in Gethsemane, we pray for the fullness of the kingdom in the sufferings of the "not yet." In Jesus, we live expectantly in the knowledge of his risen presence. Yet, in these "in between" times, we are a people who wait. Jesus gives us a prayer to support us in our waiting.

Our prayer is for "food, forgiveness, and freedom from evil" (52, p. 61). We pray for bread, but not only for the bread of daily sustenance. We ask for and receive eucharistic bread, which sustains us in our time of waiting and anticipates the banquet celebration of Omega.

We pray for forgiveness. We are a community bonded in unconditional love and reconciliation. As we receive and mediate God's gracious forgiveness, we participate in God's ongoing creation and healing of the world.

We pray for freedom from the power of sin, which the apocalyptic clash between goodness and evil unleashed. Trusting, we receive the strength and the courage to make the prayer of Jesus the reality of our own self-surrender.

Suggested Approach to Prayer: Our Father

- **Daily Prayer Pattern:**
  I quiet myself and relax in the presence of God.
  I declare my dependence on God.

- **Grace:**

I ask to enter with Jesus into his prayer in the garden, to share his surrender to the Father.

- **Method:** Meditative Reading

I enter into the garden with Jesus. I sit beside him and quietly begin to pray the Our Father. Beginning with the word "Father," I remain with each word of the prayer, gently repeating it for as long a time as it speaks to me, for as long as it touches me interiorly.

I proceed this way throughout the text of the prayer. If any word or phrase seems particularly fruitful, I rest with its resonance, allowing myself to absorb the fullness of its direction and/or consolation.

- **Closing:**

I let my heart speak simply, openly to Jesus.
I pray the Our Father.

- **Review of Prayer:**

I record in my journal whatever insights and feelings have surfaced during my prayer.

Week Three, Day 3 | The Kiss

Matthew 26:47-56

> *While he was still speaking, Judas, one of the twelve, arrived; with him was a large crowd with swords and clubs, from the chief priests and the elders of the people. Now the betrayer had given them a sign, saying, "The one I will kiss is the man; arrest him." At once he came up to Jesus and said, "Greetings, Rabbi!" and kissed him. Jesus said to him, "Friend, do what you are here to do." Then they came and laid hands on Jesus and arrested him. Suddenly, one of those with Jesus put his hand on his sword, drew it, and struck the slave of the high priest, cutting off his ear. Then Jesus said to him, "Put your sword back into its place; for all who take the sword will perish by the sword. Do you think that I cannot appeal to my Father, and he will at once send me more than twelve legions of angels? But how then would the scriptures be fulfilled, which say it must happen in this way?" At that hour Jesus said to the crowds, "Have you come out with swords and clubs to arrest me as though I were a bandit? Day after day I sat in the temple teaching, and you did not arrest me. But all this has taken place, so that the scriptures of the prophets may be fulfilled." Then all the disciples deserted him and fled.*

Commentary

In the darkness, a kiss calls forth surrender and new life. In the garden of Eden God breathed the breath of life into Adam, and he became a living spirit (Genesis 2:7). In the garden of Gethsemane the breath of a kiss initiated the surrender that released into the entire world the compassionate spirit of Jesus.

In the surrender of Jesus to God, *all* history and *all* prophecy will find fulfillment. Just as, in the beginning, God's creative spirit hovered over the chaos (Genesis 1:2), God's creative spirit is now present and active in darkness, in the confusion and anguish of human sinfulness and betrayal.

Who gave this kiss to Jesus? It was one of his own, a disciple whom he taught and loved, a friend with whom he shared his life. Only such a loved one could have the power and the authority to seize, to hold, and to identify him.

It was Judas Iscariot. Though little is actually known about Judas and his motivation, legend invests his character with a definitive—though perhaps unwarranted—degree of evil.

Dante, for example, places Judas in the pit of hell, at the lowest level of degradation. Along with the traitors Brutus and Cassius, he depicts Judas dangling from one of the mouths of Satan! (3, *Inferno*, canto 34, lines 60ff). Others who are somewhat more benevolent suggest that Judas, as a member of the Zealots, was disappointed in Jesus and collaborated with the enemy from a miscalculated hope of forcing Jesus to action.

The truth lies not in making Judas the personification of evil or in justifying his actions and thereby excusing him of responsibility. The human personality is too complex for such simplistic judgments.

We cannot underestimate, however, the significance of the person of Judas, of his presence and action, at this juncture in Jesus' life. Moreover, Judas' character and actions mirror the potential for evil and betrayal that lurks in our own inner darkness. Judas' betrayal of Jesus brings us face to face with the dark side of our selves. Examining it challenges us to greater awareness of how we betray our God, ourselves, and each other.

Judas' betrayal was not the only betrayal Jesus experienced that night in the garden. Peter, as well as each of the other apostles, shared in the denial and desertion of their friend and mentor. What a crushing disappointment for Jesus to once again encounter his followers' fear and lack of understanding. In the critical moment, they failed to comprehend his life-giving destiny, failed to support his mission of nonresistant surrender (Isaiah 50:5).

Jesus faced his ordeal in utter aloneness.

Yet there is no fatalism, no stoicism, and no hesitancy in his decision or his actions. Jesus knew his God and he knew his destiny. Jesus was firmly grounded in the prophetic word that had shaped his people, and it sustained his heart in this hour. In the darkness of the garden, the kiss of Judas found Jesus in readiness.

Suggested Approach to Prayer: Night of Betrayal

- **Daily Prayer Pattern:**
  I quiet myself and relax in the presence of God.
  I declare my dependence on God.

- **Grace:**
  I ask God to allow me to enter into sorrow as I stay with Christ in his suffering, borne on my behalf.

- **Method:** Contemplation
  I place myself in the garden of Gethsemane. I note the darkness in the garden. I am aware of the scents and sounds of the night. . . . I am aware of the disciples who are present in the garden, of their expression and their awareness of Jesus as he turns toward the gate.
  I hear the noises of an approaching mob and see the light of their torches as they approach. As they draw nearer, I see the crude weapons they are carrying.

At the head of the mob I see Judas. I watch as he approaches Jesus and kisses him. I listen attentively to the exchange between Jesus and Judas. I become aware of my response as I listen and watch.

I see some of the soldiers come forward to arrest Jesus. In the confusion that follows, I see a disciple strike one of the high priest's servants with a sword. I listen as Jesus reprimands the disciple. I take particular note of Jesus' facial expression and the tone of his voice during this episode. I continue to listen to Jesus as he speaks to the crowd.

As Jesus is arrested and led away, I am aware of how alone he is, that all his disciples have fled. With the disciples, I ponder, "How have I betrayed Jesus?"

- **Closing:**
  I speak to Jesus of my love and my gratitude for his love.
  I close my prayer with the Our Father.

- **Review of Prayer:**
  I record in my journal my feeling responses and any new insights that have surfaced during this period of prayer.

Week Three, Day 4 | The Night Before

Luke 22:54-65

> *They seized him and led him away, bringing him into the high priest's house. But Peter was following at a distance. When they had kindled a fire in the middle of the courtyard and sat down together, Peter sat among them. Then a servant-girl, seeing him in the firelight, stared at him and said, "This man also was with him." But he denied it, saying, "Woman, I do not know him." A little later someone else, on seeing him, said, "You also are one of them." But Peter said, "Man, I am not!" Then about an hour later still another kept insisting, "Surely this man also was with him; for he is a Galilean." But Peter said, "Man, I do not know what you are talking about!" At that moment, while he was still speaking, the cock crowed. The Lord turned and looked at Peter. Then Peter remembered the word of the Lord, how he had said to him, "Before the cock crows today, you will deny me three times." And he went out and wept bitterly.*

> *Now the men who were holding Jesus began to mock him and beat him; they also blindfolded him and kept asking him, "Prophesy! Who is it that struck you?" They kept heaping many other insults on him.*

Commentary

Jerusalem sleeps. Within the dark bowels of its night, a restlessness of hatred, irrationality, and fear ignites and tests all those within the deceptive warmth of its blaze.

It is into this enemy territory, to the house of the high priest, that Jesus is taken. After subjecting Jesus to a preliminary and illegal hearing, the priests and elders turn him over to a band of underlings who are to guard him through the night until morning when he will be tried and convicted.

In the outer courtyard a fire has been lit. It provides both heat and light, and draws all present into its circle. The gathering does not reflect, however, a campfire congeniality. Rather, the atmosphere is one of vulgarity and feverish agitation. It is a night void of all propriety and restriction, a Mardi Gras before Ash Wednesday. The guards seize the opportunity of their happenstance authority over Jesus to vent their abhorrent humor in the primitive cruelty of mockery and abuse.

Jesus, the prophet, the one whose eyes have looked with penetrating love into the souls of men and women, is subjected to the humiliating blindfold game of "guess who."

Among those who mill around the fire is one who has known that look of love. That one is Peter, trusted disciple and close friend of Jesus. Peter has followed Jesus to this place, unaware that here will be his own time of greatest testing. Passionate in his declarations to follow Christ even to death, Peter is not without courage (Luke 22:33). It is, in fact, this confident courage that makes him so vulnerable to his own limitations.

And he fails! After three years of faithful companionship in the company of Jesus, three years of struggle and growth, Peter, in a fear-filled moment of weakness, denies his relationship with Jesus. Peter denies Jesus not once, but three times. He vows that he does not even know Jesus, and he likewise denies any association with the other disciples. His betrayal is a callous repudiation of the one thing that had given his life its greatest meaning.

"The Lord turned and looked at Peter." Peter sees not anger, but heart-break in Jesus' face.

And Peter "wept bitterly." Recognition of his overconfidence and base guilt plunges Peter's heart into grief. In the darkness Peter weeps bitterly, sustained only by memories of Jesus' prayer and promise (Luke 22:62).

Near the dying embers in the courtyard, Jesus waits. He had said, "I came to bring fire to the earth, and how I wish it were already kindled! I have a baptism with which to be baptized, and what stress I am under until it is completed!" (Luke 12:49-50).

It has begun.

Suggested Approach to Prayer: The Look of Jesus

• **Daily Prayer Pattern:**
  I quiet myself and relax in the presence of God.
  I declare my dependence on God.

• **Grace:**
  I ask God to allow me to enter into sorrow as I stay with Christ in his suffering, borne on my behalf and because of my sins.

• **Method:** Contemplation
  I find myself in the courtyard of the house of Annas. I approach and feel the heat from the fire in the center of the courtyard. I am aware of the guards and servants who are present, and I watch their actions and listen to them. I pay particular attention to the feeling that charges the atmosphere.

  At one side I see Jesus, held prisoner by the guards. I become aware of his responses as the guards blindfold him and begin their taunting.

My attention shifts to Peter. I see his reaction to the situation and watch as the servants question him. I listen and watch sensitively as Peter denies Jesus and fellowship with the other disciples.

I hear the cock crow. I see Jesus turn toward Peter. I allow myself time to fully absorb Jesus' look at Peter. I allow myself to receive the look of Jesus as he turns to me.

- **Closing:**

I speak with Jesus, sharing with him my sorrow for my denials of him, my gratitude for his unconditional love.

I close with the Our Father.

- **Review of Prayer:**

I record in my journal whatever insights or feelings have surfaced during my period of prayer.

Week Three, Day 5 | The Bound Prisoner

Luke 22:66—23:1

> *When day came, the assembly of the elders of the people, both chief priests and scribes, gathered together, and they brought him to their council. They said, "If you are the Messiah, tell us." He replied, "If I tell you, you will not believe; and if I question you, you will not answer. But from now on the Son of Man will be seated at the right hand of the power of God." All of them asked, "Are you, then, the Son of God?" He said to them, "You say that I am." Then they said, "What further testimony do we need? We have heard it ourselves from his own lips!"*
>
> *Then the assembly rose as a body and brought Jesus before Pilate.*

Commentary

The swaddled child of Bethlehem has become the bound prisoner before the Sanhedrin. During the stillness of a tranquil Bethlehem night, in a cave which served as a manger, a woman gave birth to a son. From nearby fields, shepherds came. Filled with faith, they came to see the child whose birth had long been promised. Overjoyed at the sight of the child with his mother, the shepherds proclaimed that this child was, for all, the long-awaited realization of their hope, "Christ the Lord."

The swaddled child has become the bound prisoner. In the predawn of a Jerusalem morning, the supreme council of official Judaism convenes. Projecting a façade of legal formality, the seventy members of the Sanhedrin are seated in a semicircle. Within the council, the Sadducees and Pharisees, long-time enemies, have found a common focus for their hostility.

"If you are the Messiah, tell us." Contempt and prejudice are palpable as the council members vindictively direct charges toward their victim. At last, they have apprehended the one whom the people proclaim to be their promised Messiah. The one whose presence they perceive as a threat to their power and influence stands before them.

How can this be? The one proclaimed by God's angel to be the Son of God (Luke 1:32-35), the one whom God identified as his chosen one, his beloved Son (3:22), is now charged with claiming that sonship.

"Are you, then, the Son of God?"

How can this be? Those who level the charge are the ones who publicly invest him with his identity!

"You say that I am."

Those who were to judge now become the judged. In the presence of Jesus, official Judaism is confronted with the reality that fulfills yet transcends it. Blinded in leadership, the members of the Sanhedrin are closed to the new paradigm Jesus offers. They ask the question but cannot hear the answer.

Jesus, however, is tranquil, confident of his innocence, and trusting in God. He is, indeed, the Christ, Son of God and Son of Man! "From now on," present to the church, "seated at the right hand of . . . God," he is the source of transforming power.

Jesus' response to the Sanhedrin goes far beyond their questioning. His suffering transcends all history; his Spirit transforms all time. The bound prisoner has become the source of liberation for all!

Suggested Approach to Prayer: Lord Jesus Christ

- **Daily Prayer Pattern:**
  I quiet myself and relax in the presence of God.
  I declare my dependence on God.

- **Grace:**
  I ask God to allow me to enter into sorrow as I stay with Christ in his suffering, borne on my behalf and because of my sins.

- **Method:** Repeated Prayer
  I relax and center deep within myself. I spiral downward to discover where it is that I most experience myself bound and unfree.
  Aware of my own lack of freedom, I recite slowly and repeatedly the prayer, "Lord Jesus Christ, Son of the living God, have mercy on me, a sinner."

- **Closing:** (Review the Colloquy section on p. 21.)
  I close my prayer by resting in Jesus' spirit of merciful love.
  I pray the Our Father.

- **Review of Prayer:**
  I record in my journal whatever insight or feelings have surfaced during my period of prayer.

Week Three, Day 6 | Repetition

Suggested Approach to Prayer

- **Daily Prayer Pattern:**
  I quiet myself and relax in the presence of God.
  I declare my dependence on God.

- **Grace:**
  I ask God to allow me to enter into sorrow as I stay with Christ in his suffering, borne on my behalf and because of my sins.

- **Method:** Repetition
  In preparation, I review my prayer periods since the last repetition day. I select for my repetition the period of prayer in which I was most deeply moved or the one in which I experienced a lack of emotional response, or one in which I was grasped with insight or experienced confusion. I use the method with which I approached the passage initially. I open myself to hear again God's word to me in that particular passage.

- **Review of Prayer:**
  I write in my journal any feelings, experiences, or insights that have surfaced in this "second listening."

Today You Will Be with Me in Paradise

Week Four, Day 1 | Suffered under Pontius Pilate

Matthew 27:11-25

Jesus stood before the governor; and the governor asked him, "Are you the King of the Jews?" Jesus said, "You say so." But when he was accused by the chief priests and elders, he did not answer. Then Pilate said to him, "Do you not hear how many accusations they make against you?" But he gave him no answer, not even to a single charge, so that the governor was greatly amazed.

Now at the festival the governor was accustomed to release a prisoner for the crowd, anyone whom they wanted. At that time they had a notorious prisoner, called Jesus Barabbas. So after they had gathered, Pilate said to them, "Whom do you want me to release for you, Jesus Barabbas or Jesus who is called the Messiah?" For he realized that it was out of jealousy that they had handed him over. While he was sitting on the judgment seat, his wife sent word to him, "Have nothing to do with that innocent man, for today I have suffered a great deal because of a dream about him." Now the chief priests and the elders persuaded the crowds to ask for Barabbas and to have Jesus killed. The governor again said to them, "Which of the two do you want me to release for you?" And they said, "Barabbas." Pilate said to them, "Then what should I do with Jesus who is called the Messiah?" All of them said, "Let him be crucified!" Then he asked, "Why, what evil has he done?" But they shouted all the more, "Let him be crucified!"

So when Pilate saw that he could do nothing, but rather that a riot was beginning, he took some water and washed his hands before the crowd, saying, "I am innocent of this man's blood; see to it yourselves." Then the people as a whole answered, "His blood be on us and on our children!"

Commentary

"I found myself in a dim room" she began, "where a great number of people were assembled and appeared to be praying; but their words passed by me like murmuring water. Then, suddenly, it seemed as though my ears opened wide or as though the jet of a fountain were leaping from dark waters, and I heard distinctly the words, 'suffered under Pontius Pilate, was crucified, died and was buried.' I could not explain it to myself how my husband's name had come to be upon the lips of these people, nor what it might mean. Nevertheless, I felt an undefined dread upon hearing these words, as though they could have no other but some mysterious and ominous significance" (76, pp. 10–11).

Gertrud von le Fort has imaginatively recreated the terror and panic that grips Claudia, the wife of Pilate, when she awakens from a dream in which she has seen future generations of people all praying the words of the creed. Passing through the churches and cathedrals down the ages, Claudia hears, repeated over and over, her husband's guilt, "suffered under Pontius Pilate, . . ." and is appalled. The foreboding message of this dream moves her to send an urgent warning to Pilate, "Don't have anything to do with that innocent man."

His wife's warning comes to Pilate as he sits on the seat of judgment. Pilate's interrogation of Jesus is complete; the ingeniousness of Jesus' non-committal responses has become obvious in the questioning. To Pilate's question, "Are you the king of the Jews?" Jesus' answer ambiguously affirms his messiahship.

Convinced of Jesus' innocence and believing that he is the victim of the Sanhedrin's envy, Pilate is inclined to set Jesus free, and Claudia's warning only reinforces his conviction. In response to the formal charges of treason brought by the Jewish leaders, however, Jesus is silent.

Jesus' silence is significant in shaping the events that bring him to the cross. That silence stymies Pilate's efforts to release Jesus, and in the end, Pilate desperately turns to the crowd of pilgrims who fill the city for the celebration of Passover.

Despite the pervasive attitude of distrust and political unrest, Pilate appeals to the integrity of the people. Confident that they will choose Jesus, he invokes the custom of releasing a prisoner at Passover. He presents them with a choice between Jesus of Nazareth and a notorious terrorist, Barabbas. To his dismay, the crowd, swayed by the priests and elders, shout for the release of Barabbas. Pilate is caught between his own conviction of Jesus' innocence and the crowd's irrational choice of Barabbas.

The crowd's hostility rises to new heights when Pilate questions them. Their fury mounts to the brink of riot as they explosively demand the most brutal form of Roman execution, crucifixion, for Jesus.

Yielding to the pressure of the mob, Pilate chooses an illusion of peace over simple justice. At the crossroads of critical decision, threatened by the radical message and way of Jesus, both Jew and gentile capitulate to political expediency.

There is a nightmarish, Lady Macbeth quality in Pilate's attempt to purge himself of guilt by the ritual washing of his hands. There is a grim and enduring tragedy in the people's arrogant assumption of Jesus' guilt. There is deep sadness in the death of Jesus, who was humiliated and rejected, "like a sheep that before its shearers is silent, so he did not open his mouth" (Isaiah 53:7).

He suffered under Pontius Pilate. . . .

Suggested Approach to Prayer: The Creed

- **Daily Prayer Pattern:**
  I quiet myself and relax in the presence of God.
  I declare my dependence on God.

- **Grace:**
  I ask for the gift of being able to feel sorrow with Christ in sorrow, to be anguished with Christ's anguish, and even to experience tears and deep grief because of all the affliction Christ has endured for me.

- **Method:** Meditative Reading
  I imagine myself in a great cathedral, one of the many people who have made up the Christian community throughout the ages. I join my voice to those of the great choir as I pray slowly and meditatively the words of the Apostles' Creed.

  Beginning with the words "I believe in God," I remain with each word of the prayer, gently repeating it for as long as it speaks to me, for as long as it touches me interiorly.

  I continue this way through the text of the prayer. If any word or phrase seems particularly fruitful, I rest with its resonance, allowing myself to absorb the fullness of its direction and/or consolation.

The Apostles' Creed

I believe in God, the Father almighty, creator of heaven and earth; I believe in Jesus Christ, His only Son, Our Lord. He was conceived by the power of the Holy Spirit and born of the Virgin Mary. He suffered under Pontius Pilate, was crucified, died, and was buried. He descended to the dead. On the third day he rose again. He ascended into heaven, and is seated at the right hand of the Father. He will come again to judge the living and the dead. I believe in the Holy Spirit, the holy catholic church, the communion of saints, the forgiveness of sins, the resurrection of the body, and life everlasting. Amen.

- **Closing:**
  I allow my heart to speak simply, openly to Jesus.
  I pray the Our Father.

- **Review of Prayer:**
  I record in my journal the feelings and insights that have surfaced during my prayer period.

Week Four, Day 2 | Silent before Herod

Luke 23:6-12

> *When Pilate heard this, he asked whether the man was a Galilean. And when he learned that he was under Herod's jurisdiction, he sent him off to Herod, who was himself in Jerusalem at that time. When Herod saw Jesus, he was very glad, for he had been wanting to see him for a long time, because he had heard about him and was hoping to see him perform some sign. He questioned him at some length, but Jesus gave him no answer. The chief priests and the scribes stood by, vehemently accusing him. Even Herod with his soldiers treated him with contempt and mocked him; then he put an elegant robe on him, and sent him back to Pilate. That same day Herod and Pilate became friends with each other; before this they had been enemies.*

Commentary

"Jesus gave him no answer." Jesus is silent; he is alone.

With each episode of his passion, as Jesus moves into his "hour," we see him become increasingly more isolated and silent. He stands before Herod utterly without support. His disciples have deserted him, his own people have rejected him, and God is silent.

Again Jesus faces accusations and questions. He is silent. He is innocent. There is no evidence to substantiate any wrongdoing. There is no defense for guiltlessness. To answer the questions of his accusers would be to betray who he is, who his God is, and the significance of this moment.

The moment calls for surrender and trust. Anything less than total acceptance would violate the integrity of his life and the absolute primacy of God. Silence is his only response. Jesus is self-assured and composed in the situation. His silence is the strongest rebuke he can give to Herod.

Whatever Pilate's reasons for sending Jesus to Herod—whether from fear, or to flatter Herod, or simply to rid himself of Jesus—Herod is filled only with curiosity and contempt. Refusing to take Jesus seriously, Herod makes a joke of the incident.

Herod is unable to prove or disprove the accusations against Jesus, and after he and his soldiers have had "their fun," Herod sends Jesus back to Pilate robed in a ceremonial cloak. Ironically, the garment is less a statement of mockery and guilt than it is an eloquent sign of Jesus' innocence. Neither Herod nor Pilate can prove Jesus guilty, and neither can release him. In the mutuality of their powerlessness they forge a tenuous bond.

The passion of Jesus continues to unfold. Progressively, he is more alone, more silent. As he approaches his final surrender, the silence of Jesus encounters ever more deeply the silence of God (46, p. 181).

Suggested Approach to Prayer: Entry into Silence

- **Daily Prayer Pattern:**
  I quiet myself and relax in the presence of God.
  I declare my dependence on God.

- **Grace:**
  I ask for the gift of being able to feel sorrow with Christ in sorrow, to be anguished with Christ's anguish, and even to experience tears and deep grief because of all the afflictions Christ has endured for me.

- **Method:** Contemplation

I see Jesus as he is brought before Herod. I try to picture, in detail, the palace room in which they meet. I am aware of how Jesus' dress and demeanor are in sharp contrast with Herod and his surroundings.

I look at Herod and note his facial expression as he meets Christ and proceeds to question him. I take note of the tone of his questions—anger, curiosity, malice. I see the chief priests and scribes who are present and listen to their violent accusations. I observe Jesus' face as he is subjected to the interrogation and accusations. I see Jesus silent.

I enter into the silence of Jesus as into a room of deep quiet and stillness. I allow myself to surrender to this silence.

As far as I am able, I allow the experience of the silence to be given expression through my five senses, asking myself, "What color or hue is the mood of Jesus' silence? What is the 'sound' of this silence . . . the scent? What does this silence taste like, feel like?" I allow the silence of Jesus to fill my whole being.

- **Closing:**

I speak with Jesus and stay with him through everything that happens. I close the period of prayer with the Our Father.

- **Review of Prayer:**

I record in my journal the feelings and insights that have surfaced during my prayer.

Week Four, Day 3 | Truth on Trial

John 18:33-38; 19:1-12

Then Pilate entered the headquarters again, summoned Jesus, and asked him, "Are you the King of the Jews?" Jesus answered, "Do you ask this on your own, or did others tell you about me?" Pilate replied, "I am not a Jew, am I? Your own nation and the chief priests have handed you over to me. What have you done?" Jesus answered, "My kingdom is not from this world. If my kingdom were from this world, my followers would be fighting to keep me from being handed over to the Jews. But as it is, my kingdom is not from here." Pilate asked him, "So you are a king?" Jesus answered, "You say that I am a king. For this I was born, and for this I came into the world, to testify to the truth. Everyone who belongs to the truth listens to my voice." Pilate asked him, "What is truth?" After he had said this, he went out to the Jews again and told them, "I find no case against him."

Then Pilate took Jesus and had him flogged. And the soldiers wove a crown of thorns and put it on his head, and they dressed him in a purple robe. They kept coming up to him, saying, "Hail, King of the Jews!" and striking him on the face. Pilate went out again and said to them, "Look, I am bringing him out to you to let you know that I find no case against him." So Jesus came out, wearing the crown of thorns and the purple robe. Pilate said to them, "Here is the man!" When the chief priests and the police saw him, they shouted, "Crucify him! Crucify him!" Pilate said to them, "Take him yourselves and crucify him; I find no case against him." The Jews answered him, "We have a law, and according to that law he ought to die because he has claimed to be the Son of God."

Now when Pilate heard this, he was more afraid than ever. He entered his headquarters again and asked Jesus, "Where are you from?" But Jesus gave him no answer. Pilate therefore said to him, "Do you refuse to speak to me? Do you not know that I have power to release you, and power to crucify you?" Jesus answered him, "You would have no power over me unless it had been given you from above; therefore the one who handed me over to you is guilty of a greater sin." From then on Pilate tried to release him, but the Jews cried out, "If you release this man, you are no friend of the emperor. Everyone who claims to be a king sets himself against the emperor."

Commentary

A king is crowned! A king is robed in regal glory! Subjects render their master homage and praise!

His crown is a bloody diadem of twisted thorns, sharply pressed into the flesh of his scalp. His robe is a common cloak of a soldier, worn and faded. The "homage" he receives is accompanied, contemptuously, by slapping blows.

Ironically, this vulgar mimicry of a royal investiture speaks a profound truth. A king *is* crowned!

The soldiers' grotesque parody serves, unconsciously, to unveil the truth that some of the Jews reject and Pilate compromises. In spite of their ignorance, the soldiers do, in reality, declare the kingship of Christ.

Pilate alone appears to recognize Jesus' innocence. Searching for a reason to release him, Pilate is puzzled by Jesus' words and overwhelmed by Jesus' silence.

Yet in the end, Pilate's incompetent leadership gets the better of him. Marked by years of unsympathetic treatment of the Jewish people and their beliefs, Pilate's position as governor is in constant jeopardy as the people of Judea wait in alertness to report his next false step to Rome. So, in fear of losing his position as governor if a riot were to break out, Pilate abandons the truth, yielding instead to political expediency and the wishes of the mob.

Pilate is caught in a trap of his own making, in a dilemma of powerlessness. Deeply rooted fear and insecurity prevent him from acting in truth. His spirit dulled and calloused by years of insensitivity, Pilate surrenders Jesus to death.

The travesty of this trial ends as it began, with the cruel parody of a royal acclamation "Here is your king" (John 19:14). Pilate rejects the man who said, "I am . . . the truth" (14:6). Once more, in ignorance, truth is spoken.

Standing vulnerably before the rabble, scourged and humiliated, the man Jesus *is* king. His truth and his witness to truth are our entrance into the kingdom.

The power of the kingdom is the spirit of the risen Christ seen in the strength of truth as it continues to break through human limitation and sin. From the cross of Christ, the words of Pilate, written two thousand years ago, proclaim today the truth at the heart of all human history, "Jesus of Nazareth, the King of the Jews" (John 19:19).

Suggested Approach to Prayer: Jesus, Mocked and Rejected

- **Daily Prayer Pattern:**
  I quiet myself and relax in the presence of God.
  I declare my dependence on God.

- **Grace:**
  I ask for the gift to be able to feel sorrow with Christ in sorrow, to be anguished with Christ's anguish, and even to experience tears and deep grief because of all the afflictions Christ has endured for me.

- **Method:** Contemplation
  Slowly and prayerfully I reread the passage. I choose one person in the passage whose role I will assume, perhaps a soldier or someone in the crowd.

  I picture the city of Jerusalem, its streets filled with the milling crowds who have come to celebrate Passover. I see the crowd that has assembled near the Praetorium, where Pilate is conducting his interrogation of Jesus. I picture the building, the details of its architecture, the flagstone terrace, the arched gates. . . .

  Intently, I look at Pilate. I take note of his clothing, which symbolizes his office. I am aware of how his physical bearing reveals his inner attitude, and I listen as he questions Jesus, aware of the tone of his interrogation.

  "Are you the king of the Jews?" I closely observe Jesus as he makes his response. I am aware of how his silence and response deeply reveal the truth.

  As the people scream out for Barabbas, I note the expression on Jesus' face. I go with Jesus as he is taken away to be scourged, and I am present as the soldiers crown him with thorns and mock him. I continue to be aware of Jesus' pain and humiliation. I follow Jesus as Pilate leads him out before the people and places him on public display.

As the dialogue between Pilate and Jesus continues, I am sensitive to the struggle within Pilate's spirit and the pathos of Jesus' rejection. I see Pilate hand Jesus over to be crucified.

• **Closing:**
I speak to Jesus and stay with him through everything that happens.
I pray the Our Father.

• **Review of Prayer:**
I write in my journal whatever feelings or insights have surfaced during this period of prayer.

Week Four, Day 4 | Good Friday Journey

John 19:13-22

When Pilate heard these words, he brought Jesus outside and sat on the judge's bench at a place called The Stone Pavement, or in Hebrew Gabbatha. Now it was the day of Preparation for the Passover; and it was about noon. He said to the Jews, "Here is your King!" They cried out, "Away with him! Away with him! Crucify him!" Pilate asked them, "Shall I crucify your King?" The chief priests answered, "We have no king but the emperor." Then he handed him over to them to be crucified.

So they took Jesus; and carrying the cross by himself, he went out to what is called The Place of the Skull, which in Hebrew is called Golgotha. There they crucified him, and with him two others, one on either side, with Jesus between them. Pilate also had an inscription written and put on the cross. It read, "Jesus of Nazareth, the King of the Jews." Many of the Jews read this inscription, because the place where Jesus was crucified was near the city; and it was written in Hebrew, in Latin, and in Greek. Then the chief priests of the Jews said to Pilate, "Do not write, 'The King of the Jews,' but, 'This man said, I am King of the Jews.'" Pilate answered, "What I have written I have written."

Commentary

Thousands of women, men, and children make their way along the narrow streets of old Jerusalem. Some are singing, some are praying aloud, and some walk in total silence. The day is Good Friday.

Around the earth in churches everywhere on Good Friday, people make an imaginary journey down these same streets. Whether in the streets of Jerusalem or in the aisles of a church, all these people carry within their hearts a vision of holiness, the *mysterium tremendum*, and *mysterium fascinans* (24, p. 9). It is a vision so gripping that one is simultaneously repelled by it and drawn into it. In these gatherings each one knows that he or she has an intimate share in the drama that is unfolding. That drama is *the way of the cross*.

"Good" Friday is the time when Christian people come before the crucified Jesus. They come with a deep desire to discover within his suffering a meaning for their own brokenness and that of the world around them. As they, in spirit, accompany Jesus on the way to Calvary, they are aware of the weight of his cross. Just as Isaac, the beloved son, carried wood for his own sacrifice (Genesis 22:1-8), so, too, Jesus carries the heavy cross of his own sacrifice.

As the people enter into the way of the cross, they encounter in prayer the long history of promise and prophecy that Jesus' life embodies. The event is Passover, the annual celebration of the liberation of the Hebrew nation from the bondage of Egypt. Significantly, Jesus' life is handed over at the precise hour that the Passover lambs were killed in the Temple. At that hour, the Jewish people recalled how, twelve hundred years before, at the first Passover, the blood of a sacrificed lamb marked the doors of their ancestors, who were spared from death.

Now, in the surrender of Jesus, we see the new Passover, the passage of Jesus through death into new life. He is "like a lamb that is led to the slaughter" (Isaiah 53:7).

St. Teresa of Avila counsels us to "fix our eyes on the crucified" (77, p. 196). Here the Christian discovers that the endurance and faithfulness of Jesus to his role and mission is the transforming power that enables his followers to carry their own particular cross.

The words of St. Paul are further encouragement:

> We are afflicted in every way, but not crushed; perplexed, but not driven to despair; persecuted, but not forsaken; struck down, but not destroyed; always carrying in the body the death of Jesus, so that the life of Jesus may also be made visible in our bodies. For while we live, we are always being given up to death for Jesus' sake, so that the life of Jesus may be made visible in our mortal flesh, . . . because we know that the one who raised the Lord Jesus will raise us also with Jesus, and will bring us with you into his presence. (2 Corinthians 4:8-11, 14)

Suggested Approach to Prayer: The Way of the Cross

• **Daily Prayer Pattern:**
   I quiet myself and relax in the presence of God.
   I declare my dependence on God.

• **Grace:**
   I ask for the gift to be able to feel sorrow with Christ in his sorrow, to be anguished with Christ's anguish, and even to experience tears and deep grief because of all the afflictions Christ has endured for me.

- **Method:** Meditation

Using the exercise The Way of the Cross (below), I enter into the journey of Jesus from his presence before Pilate to Calvary and even to the empty tomb of Easter morning. I bring to the sufferings of Jesus my own sharing of pain, so that "in my flesh I am completing what is lacking in Christ's afflictions for the sake of his body, the church" (Colossians 1:24).

- **Closing:** (Review the Colloquy section on p. 21)

I simply stay with Jesus in silence and speak to him from my heart.

- **Review of Prayer:**

In my journal, I record the "station" that has most touched me in this prayer.

- **The Way of the Cross**

1. As Jesus appears before Pilate, I remember a time when I experienced being misunderstood, condemned.

2. As Jesus receives his cross, I recall a time when I received a cross in my life.

3. As Jesus falls the first time, I remember when I first experienced failure, my own limits.

4. As Mary encourages Jesus, I remember someone who encouraged me to follow God's call; I remember how she or he looked at me.

5. As Simon helps Jesus carry his cross, I consider who has been there to lift the cross from my shoulders, from my heart.

6. As Veronica wipes the face of Jesus, I remember the Veronicas in my life—those who stood by me, comforted me, even at the risk of their own rejection.

7. As Jesus falls a second time, I recall the times when I have experienced the helplessness of falling, knowing that I would fall again.

8. As the women reach out to comfort Jesus, I remember the faces of those whom I have reached out to comfort, even in my own pain.

9. As Jesus falls a third time, I recall a time when I felt as if I had fallen and could not go on.

10. As Jesus is stripped of his clothing, I remember the experience of feeling so poor, so stripped, so vulnerable before others.

11. As I see Jesus nailed to the cross, I consider what it is that fastens me to the cross of Jesus Christ.

12. As I contemplate Jesus dying on the cross, I recall the circumstances, the interior call to love unconditionally, to be forgiving even when there seems to be no return.

13. As I imagine Mary holding the dead body of her Son, I hold in loving memory those who received me in my pain and grieved with me.

14. As Jesus' body is laid in the tomb, I consider what it is in my life that most holds me entombed, where I most experience death.

15. As I become aware of the empty tomb of Easter morning, I am aware not only of the pain in my life, but of the new life emerging and deepening within me.

Week Four, Day 5 | King and Priest

John 19:23-24

> *When the soldiers had crucified Jesus, they took his clothes and divided them into four parts, one for each soldier. They also took his tunic; now the tunic was seamless, woven in one piece from the top. So they said to one another, "Let us not tear it, but cast lots for it to see who will get it." This was to fulfill what the scripture says,*
> > *"They divided my clothes among themselves, and for my clothing they cast lots."*

Commentary

"In his body lives the totem spirit of the tribe" (75, p. 37). These words surely can be applied to Jesus. For Jesus, as king *and* priest, embodies the life of his people, God's own Spirit.

In his crucifixion, Jesus is flagrantly displayed! Above his head the title "King of the Jews" simultaneously extols and condemns him, while at his feet, soldiers gamble to see who will win the priestlike garment, his seamless tunic.

Suspended in stark vulnerability between heaven and earth, Jesus—king and priest—unites the secular and the sacred, chaos and cosmos, creator and creature, feminine and masculine, body and spirit. Wounded, Jesus is the healer of all that is disembodied. The sufferings of Jesus are the means by which all things are reconciled to each other and to God. Through the cross, the *conjunctio oppositorum*, the marriage of opposites is effected.

In Jesus, all of humanity is thrust forward out of its slumbering darkness into the awakening of holy consciousness. "Night is truly blessed when heaven is wedded to earth and [all] is reconciled with God!" (54, Easter Vigil, p. 184).

Suggested Approach to Prayer: Before the Cross

- **Daily Prayer Pattern:**
  I quiet myself and relax in the presence of God.
  I declare my dependence on God.

- **Grace:**
  I ask for the gift to be able to feel sorrow with Christ in his sorrow, to be anguished with Christ's anguish, and even to experience tears and deep grief because of all the afflictions Christ has endured for me.

- **Method:** Contemplation
  I take my cross or crucifix in my hands and look at it closely. I see Jesus hanging there before me.
  I see the title above his head, "King of the Jews."
  I follow the outline of his body and try to imagine the suffering he endured for me. I look at his head and face, pierced by the crown of thorns. I contemplate the excruciating pain of the nails driven through his hands and feet, as they support the weight of his body. I see the lance pierce his side.
  I am aware of the starkness of his nakedness.
  I remain with Jesus in his vulnerability, taking note of the feelings that surface within me.

- **Closing:**

I allow my heart to speak to Jesus, king and priest, in my own words, or through a prayer such as, "Lord Jesus Christ, king and priest, receive my spirit."

I pray the Our Father.

- **Review of Prayer:**

I note in my journal whatever feelings or insights have surfaced during this time of prayer.

Week Four, Day 6 | Repetition

Suggested Approach to Prayer

- **Daily Prayer Pattern:**
  I quiet myself and relax in the presence of God.
  I declare my dependence on God.

- **Grace:**
  I ask God to allow me to enter into sorrow as I stay with Christ in his suffering, borne on my behalf and because of my sins.

- **Method:** Repetition
  In preparation, I review my prayer periods since the last repetition day. I select for my repetition the period of prayer in which I was most deeply moved or the one in which I experienced a lack of emotional response, or one in which I was grasped with insight or experienced confusion. I use the method with which I approached the passage initially. I open myself to hear again God's word to me in that particular passage.

- **Review of Prayer:**
  I write in my journal any feelings, experiences, or insights that have surfaced during this "second listening."

My God, My God, Why Have You Forsaken Me?

Week Five, Day 1 | Stretched between Opposites

Luke 23:39-43

> *One of the criminals who were hanged there kept deriding him and saying, "Are you not the Messiah? Save yourself and us!" But the other rebuked him, saying, "Do you not fear God, since you are under the same sentence of condemnation? And we indeed have been condemned justly, for we are getting what we deserve for our deeds, but this man has done nothing wrong." Then he said, "Jesus, remember me when you come into your kingdom." He replied, "Truly I tell you, today you will be with me in Paradise."*

Commentary

There is an ancient Jewish saying that "man enters this world with fists clenched, as if all the world were his to own; he leaves it with hands spread open, as if he wanted to say that he no longer possessed any of the things he once cherished" (57, p. 253).

The two thieves crucified on either side of Jesus have lived their lives with clenched fists. Even so, in this, their last moment, each has a choice— to mockingly seek a reprieve, or to dare to change. At the gate of death the choice is made. In the presence of Jesus, one thief challenges, the other one believes. Between the challenger and the believer, Jesus is stretched taut!

We look at the two thieves, and we see ourselves. We see our positive side and our dark, negative side. We readily identify and claim our positive "thief." He is easy to own and to love. He is always open, sincere, trusting, and desirous to be and to do good.

The dark "thief" is not so easy to accept; in fact, he is often hidden, so well disguised that we are unable to recognize him for what he is. To acknowledge and accept these "thieves," these opposites within us, is to begin to envision a new and more complete sense of self.

To live dynamically poised between the conflicting poles within us, is, paradoxically, to experience freedom. Through the cross of Jesus, the energy of the opposites becomes channeled and transformed into power for life.

In the reality of the historical Jesus nailed to a cross, we see no longer the division of opposites. Christ crucified represents balance, oneness—the unity of the right and the left, the below and the above.

It is only through the crucified Jesus that reconciliation of opposites is possible. One thief says yes to Jesus; the other tragically rejects him. To look at Jesus crucified is to see the horror of this sin and rejection. Crucified between the two thieves, Jesus experiences this rejection—physically, psychically, and spiritually.

To fix our eyes on Jesus is to be irrevocably drawn into the passion. Through him we experience our own unique "stretching" between the "thieves," the opposites within us.

In this inner passion a new awareness of the reality of the evil within us surfaces. Focused on Jesus, however, we need not be afraid of this painful encounter. We can trust that the "rejecting thief" does not speak the last word for us.

Our "good thief" also insists on making his voice heard! His courageous yes to Jesus opens us to hear and to receive our own beauty and goodness as it seeks full expression.

This entry into our personal passion is, however, not without danger. The threat of becoming overwhelmed is very real. Upon meeting our evil side we may succumb to the temptation of despair; or, on discovering the depth of our goodness, we may yield to the seduction of self-satisfaction.

Our safety through this difficult passion-passage depends on our maintaining a concentrated stillness, which is centered in Jesus.

The ultimate word of the passion of Jesus is the word of love. The love of God for Jesus and the love of Jesus for God is the force that sustains Jesus as he hangs on the cross. This energy of love allows Jesus to reach out in his own pain to beg God's compassion not only for the confessing thief but for all those who have rejected and crucified him. "Father, forgive them; for they do not know what they are doing" (Luke 23:34).

His love knows no limits. Jesus promises the thief far more than he would have ever hoped. When the thief asks merely to be remembered, Jesus responds with unlimited love, "Today you will be with me in Paradise."

For the thief and for us, the outstretched body of Jesus is the great host of new life; his cross has become the focus of the transforming, reconciling power of love.

Suggested Approach to Prayer: Promise to Paradise

• **Daily Prayer Pattern:**
   I quiet myself and relax in the presence of God.
   I declare my dependence on God.

• **Grace:**
   I ask for the gift of being able to feel sorrow with Christ in sorrow, to be anguished with Christ's anguish, and even to experience tears and deep grief because of the afflictions Christ has endured for me.

- **Method:** Contemplation

I imagine myself at the scene of the crucifixion. I attend to the atmosphere around me—the darkness of the day, the confusion of the mob, the general mood. . . .

I note, on either side of Jesus, two others who are being crucified. I become conscious of their pain, their facial expressions, their words. I see them observe Jesus and note their opposite responses and how their inner attitudes are portrayed through their words and the tone of their voices. I note the abuse and ridicule of the one and the basic honesty and belief of the other. Prayerfully, I reflect on how these opposite responses to Jesus are present today . . . in the world and within me.

I see Jesus respond to the humble request of the one thief. Listening to Jesus' promise, I allow it to resonate deeply within me.

- **Closing:**

I stay with Jesus and speak to him from my heart.
I pray the Our Father.

- **Review of Prayer:**

I note in my journal how I experience a tension of opposites within me.

Week Five, Day 2 | From Mother to Woman

John 19:25-27

> *Standing near the cross of Jesus were his mother, and his mother's sister, Mary the wife of Clopas, and Mary Magdalene. When Jesus saw his mother and the disciple whom he loved standing beside her, he said to his mother, "Woman, here is your son." Then he said to the disciple, "Here is your mother." And from that hour the disciple took her into his own home.*

Commentary

From "mother" to "woman." Mary heard her son, who had all his life called her "Mother," now in his hour of death, address her as "Woman."

The only other time Jesus called Mary "Woman" was at the wedding feast in Cana, when she pleaded with him to respond to the bridal couple's embarrassment at having run out of wine. The he replied to her, "Woman, what concern is that to you and to me? My hour has not yet come" (John 2:4).

Jesus did, however, respond to his mother's request; he met the couple's need by turning water into wine. That transformation of water into wine was the first of Jesus' great miracles. It was a powerful sign and a promise of the joy and fulfillment that the new age of Jesus would herald.

Now, on Calvary, his hour has come; the promise is being fulfilled.

In calling his mother "Woman," Jesus symbolically names and establishes, with great dignity, her role in the new age. Jesus confirms her identity when he entrusts John, the representative of all believers, to Mary. At this moment Mary's physical motherhood of Jesus, like the water changed to wine, is transformed. From this time forward, she will be the mother of all believers, "mother of the church" (1, *Lumen Gentium,* 86, note 262).

Mary is, like the first woman, mother of all the living (Genesis 3:20). In the new creation, she is recognized as the "new Eve" (1, *Lumen Gentium,* 53, p. 88). Eve brought forth her sons in pain (Genesis 3:16). Mary, also, must suffer the agony of birthing. Her labor as mother of the church begins with the death of her son. It calls for her total surrender.

Mary stands at the foot of her son's cross. She is unable to relieve his agony. She does not completely understand the reason for his dying. Yet she stands!

In faith she remains near her son. Her steadfastness in this hour vividly recalls the faithfulness of her fiat, when she surrendered her body to God's will and made possible Jesus' birth. "Here am I, the servant of the Lord; let it be with me according to your word" (Luke 1:38).

She is the great mother in labor bringing forth the life of Jesus in the world. She is the woman who stands, in love, at the foot of every cross.

Suggested Approach to Prayer: Prayer of Mary

• **Daily Prayer Pattern:**
  I quiet myself and relax in the presence of God.
  I declare my dependence on God.

• **Grace:**
  I ask to share in the sufferings of Jesus, in the spirit of Mary.

• **Method:** Repeated Prayer
  I imagine myself with Mary at the foot of the cross. I try to visual-

ize the surroundings in great detail—for example, the time of day, the warmth or chill in the air, the people (soldiers, faithful women, Pharisees, simple onlookers). I note the expressions on their faces—perhaps curiosity, disbelief, fear, compassion, sorrow.

I look closely at Mary. I take note of the emotions that etch her face and posture. . . . I especially note how all her attention is focused on Jesus as he hangs on the cross.

I, too, look at Jesus. I look intently at the muscles of his body, stretched taut, at the nails that have cruelly pierced his flesh, at the pain in his eyes.

I see Jesus look directly into my eyes. I hear him say to me, "_____, behold your mother." I hear him say to Mary, of me, "Woman, behold your son/daughter."

Here is Mary, whose steadfast loyalty and faithfulness to Jesus serve to nurture my own faith commitment to Jesus.

I pray, repeatedly, the words of Jesus:

"_____, behold your mother. Woman, behold your son/daughter."

Here is Mary, whose surrendering yes to God nurtures the inbreaking of new creation and hope within me.

"_____, behold your mother. Woman, behold your son/daughter."

Here is Mary, whose love openly welcomes and nurtures me within the community of Christ's body, the church.

"_____, behold your mother. Woman, behold your son/daughter."

Here is Mary, whose concern for my human needs nurtures an openness to God's transforming power within me.

"_____, behold your mother. Woman, behold your son/daughter."

Here is Mary, whose willingness to stand at the foot at the cross strengthens me to risk and to endure the suffering of my particular circumstances in life, my share in her son's passion.

"_____, behold your mother. Woman, behold your son/daughter."

I continue to repeat the words of Jesus slowly and prayerfully, for as long as they continue to nourish me.

- **Closing:**

I thank Jesus for the gift of his mother, the woman who stands at the foot of the cross.

I pray the Hail Mary.

- **Review of Prayer:**

I record in my journal the images of this time of prayer that have most deeply touched me.

Week Five, Day 3 | One of Us

John 19:28-29

> *After this, when Jesus knew that all was now finished, he said (in order to fulfill the scripture), "I am thirsty." A jar full of sour wine was standing there. So they put a sponge full of the wine on a branch of hyssop and held it to his mouth.*

Commentary

"I am thirsty." Jesus' poignant cry from the cross speaks strongly to us of his humanness.

If there is any time when the humanness of Jesus is undeniably apparent, it is as he hangs on the cross. It is impossible to look at him crucified or to listen to his human cry of thirst and not realize that Jesus is radically one of us, that he, God's Son, has been "injected" into our humanness, into our world.

The amazing reality that Jesus—God's Son—actually became one of us is what enables him to do the work that the Creator has entrusted to him. That work is the unification of the world: "That they may all be one. As you, Father, are in me and I am in you, may they also be in us, so that the world may believe that you have sent me" (John 17:21).

The inner thirst of Jesus, and our thirst, too, is the deep and intense longing within each of us for this oneness with each other and oneness in God. This yearning for union is the evolutionary pull that inevitably draws all of creation upward and forward toward the new creation, the lived reality of God's presence in our world.

The cross is the symbol of hope and emergence. The suffering and death of Jesus not only heals our brokenness but transforms it, opening us in receptivity to the power of the risen Christ. Suffering overcomes all resistance to the entry of Christ's spirit within us. The cross is a profound symbol of the love-work of the Creator lived out in the struggle and pain of daily life.

This labor of love offers no escape from suffering. The Christian, like Christ, must endure the thirst for communion, which is, paradoxically, the energy of the cross.

Jesus says, "I thirst." We say, "I thirst."

> The Spirit and the bride say, "Come."
> And let everyone who hears say, "Come."
> *And let everyone who is thirsty come.*
> Let anyone who wishes *take the water of life as a gift.*
> —Revelation 22:17

Suggested Approach to Prayer: I Thirst

• **Daily Prayer Pattern:**
  I quiet myself and relax in the presence of God.
  I declare my dependence on God.

• **Grace:**
  I ask for the gift of being able to feel the inner thirst that was a poignant part of Jesus' passion.

- **Method:** Meditation

Prayerfully, I reread John 19:28-29. I imagine the thirst of Christ and hear his cry.

In answering the following questions, I bring my thirst to Christ.

"As a child, what did I thirst for? What have the experiences of my life revealed to me about my thirst? What do I want my experience of thirst to be? What does all this say to me about myself, my thirst, my journey?"

As I contemplate the thirst of Jesus, I consider how his thirst, in suffering, speaks to me and my life circumstances.

- **Closing:**

I speak to Christ and stay with him through everything that happens.
I pray the Our Father.

- **Review of Prayer:**

I note in my journal whatever feelings or insights have surfaced during my prayer.

Week Five, Day 4 | The Cross—Catalyst

Matthew 27:39-44

> *Those who passed by derided him, shaking their heads and saying, "You who would destroy the temple and build it in three days, save yourself! If you are the Son of God, come down from the cross." In the same way the chief priests also, along with the scribes and elders, were mocking him, saying, "He saved others; he cannot save himself. He is the King of Israel; let him come down from the cross now, and we will believe in him. He trusts in God; let God deliver him now, if he wants to; for he said, 'I am God's Son.'" The bandits who were crucified with him also taunted him in the same way.*

Commentary

Suffering is the meeting point between good and evil (37, p. 325). As Jesus hangs on the cross, Satan once again makes his evil presence known. The mocking and the jeering are his voice; his mouthpiece is the crowd.

During the temptations in the desert (Matthew 4:1-11), the forces of evil and good, darkness and light, encountered each other. In this last moment of Jesus' suffering and death, they again come face to face.

Jesus is not spared this last temptation: "If you are God's son, come down." The Jewish leaders who choose to oppose Jesus see his helplessness on the cross as total powerlessness. Arrogantly, they interpret this as proof that Jesus cannot be the Messiah, God's Son. They hinge their belief on his meeting their demands for a miracle: "Come down and we will believe."

Christ does not come down from the cross. He does not yield to an ego-inflating display of power. Rather, enduring the pain, he remains in his trust and obedience to his Father.

In the power of this radical trust and obedience, the true sonship of Jesus is shown. Only in the strength of such unlimited trust is Christ able to endure the intense suffering and degradation of his crucifixion.

By embracing the humiliation of human limitation, Jesus, God's Son, breaks through our resistance and enables us to surrender and be transformed. "It would have been human to have come down from the cross; it was divine to hang there" (52, p. 348). The historical cross of Jesus, the visible sign of his trust and obedience, catalyzes the release of God's power and goodness into our world.

Jesus is the working model for us as we search for meaning within the sufferings of our own lives. Jesus' surrender to the pain of the cross reassures us that our sufferings, like his, are part of the evolutionary process of all humankind. Suffering leads us, as it led Jesus, into the Easter oneness of love with each other and with God. Evil will not have the final word. As Pierre Teilhard de Chardin wrote, "The Christian is not asked to swoon in the shadow, but to climb in the light of the Cross" (71, p. 70).

Suggested Approach to Prayer: The Heart of Christ

- **Daily Prayer Pattern:**
  I quiet myself and relax in the presence of God.
  I declare my dependence on God.

- **Grace:**
  I ask for the gift to enter into the spirit of Jesus' passion, to share in the sorrow and anguish he endured for me.

- **Method:** Contemplation

I contemplate Jesus on the cross, noting his many sufferings. I hear the ridicule and the accusations hurled at him.

I focus my attention on Jesus' heart, his physical and spiritual center. In stillness, I concentrate all the energy of who I am on his heart.

Slowly I enter into the heart of Jesus as into a room. I am aware of any images or feelings that surface within me as I enter into the heart of Christ.

I ask Jesus to show me the love that prompted him to endure the sufferings and humiliations of his cross. I open myself to receive his heart of love, as Jesus shares it with me.

I focus my attention on Jesus heart, which is filled with love. Gathered within his heart I see
- all my own sufferings and joys and desires to love and be loved . . .
- all those I love—husband, wife, sisters and brothers, children, friends, parents . . .
- all those others for whom I am concerned—leaders of nations, the poor, prisoners, the homeless. . . .

I imagine the heart of Jesus at the converging point of love in which all creation is drawn into unity. I imagine the energy of this love flowing from and expanding to fill the entire world. I see the vast expanse of love-energy moving all of creation forward into a future when Christ will be all in all.

- **Closing:**

In my own words I express my gratitude to Jesus for having shared with me his vision and his love.

I pray the Our Father.

- **Review of Prayer:**

I write in my journal the insights and feelings that have surfaced during my prayer.

Week Five, Day 5 | Repetition

Suggested Approach to Prayer

• **Daily Prayer Pattern:**
  I quiet myself and relax in the presence of God.
  I declare my dependence on God.

• **Grace:**
  I ask God to allow me to enter into a sorrow as I stay with Christ in his sufferings, borne on my behalf and because of my sins.

• **Method:** Repetition
  In preparation, I review my prayer periods since the last repetition day. I select for my repetition the period of prayer in which I was most deeply moved or the one in which I experienced a lack of emotional response, or one in which I was grasped with insight or confusion. I use the method with which I approached the passage initially. I open myself again to God's word to me in that particular passage.

• **Review of Prayer:**
  I write in my journal any feelings, experiences, or insights that have surfaced in this "second listening."

Week Five, Day 6 | Cry of Distress

Matthew 27:45-50

> *From noon on, darkness came over the whole land until three in the afternoon. And about three o'clock Jesus cried with a loud voice, "Eli, Eli, lema sabachthani?" that is, "My God, my God, why have you forsaken me?" When some of the bystanders heard it, they said, "This man is calling for Elijah." At once one of them ran and got a sponge, filled it with sour wine, put it on a stick, and gave it to him to drink. But the others said, "Wait, let us see whether Elijah will come to save him." Then Jesus cried again with a loud voice and breathed his last.*

Commentary

Jesus hangs on the cross. To the world he seems a failure, cursed by the law and devoid of all visible support (Galatians 3:13).

Jesus, who reassured his followers of God's faithful and intimate presence in their lives, is now abandoned. Jesus, who performed so many miracles in God's name, is now without a sign. Jesus, who brought to others the confidence that God responds to every prayer, now hears no word.

"My God, my God, why have you forsaken me?" This anguished cry of Jesus is one of distress, not despair (10, p. 194). He is being prematurely cut off from life—his mission, seemingly, aborted. He is scorned and rejected. Insidiously, the question must have arisen, "Have I lived in vain? Am I a failure?" Darkness covers the earth and enters into his soul; the weight of the world's sin is heavy upon him.

Jesus' dying on the cross is a direct consequence of his life of total obedience. At every moment he has embraced what he discerned to be God's will for him. Now in the agony of his last moments, an appeal to God is literally wrenched from the depths of his being.

Although we cannot know exactly what Jesus felt at that moment, clearly he was not spared the totally human and intense experience of isolation that accompanies imminent death. His distress was unquestionably real!

Yet one does not cry out if one does not expect to be heard. The moment of greatest desperation gives energy to the deepest truth, "the heart being hard at bay, / is out with it" (13, "Wreck of the Deutschland," 57–58).

"Eli, Eli, lama sabachthani?" For those who do not believe, the cry of Jesus is misinterpreted and maliciously ridiculed. Those who believe know it is God to whom Jesus calls out.

"My God, my God, why have you forsaken me?"

These words recall the ancient Hebrew prayer in which the innocent sufferer simultaneously expresses distress and trust. The prayer of the psalmist is the spirit of the Christ.

> O my God, I cry by day, but you do not answer;
>   and by night, but find no rest.
> Yet you are holy,
>   enthroned on the praises of Israel.
> In you our ancestors trusted;
>   they trusted, and you delivered them.
> To you they cried, and were saved;
>   in you they trusted, and were not put to shame.
>   —Psalm 22:2-5

Suggested Approach to Prayer: Psalm 22

• **Daily Prayer Pattern:**
I quiet myself and relax in the presence of God.
I declare my dependence on God.

• **Grace:**
I ask for the gift to be able to feel sorrow with Christ in sorrow, to be anguished with Christ's anguish, and even to experience tears and deep grief because of all Christ has endured for me.

• **Method:** Meditative Reading
I imagine myself with Jesus on Calvary. I am aware of his utter aloneness, of the absence of his disciples. I see the scorn and hear the ridicule to which he is subjected. I am aware of the prevailing darkness of the day.

Looking at the face of Jesus, I become aware of the feelings portrayed in his expression. I hear Jesus' cry, and I allow it to echo within me. I am aware of the feelings that surface within me.

I pray Psalm 22 in the spirit of Jesus. I remain with each word of the psalm, gently repeating it for as long as it speaks to me, for as long as it touches me interiorly.

I proceed this way throughout the text of the psalm. If any word or phrase seems particularly fruitful, I rest with its resonance, allowing myself to absorb the fullness of its direction and/or consolation.

Psalm 22

My God, my God, why have you forsaken me?
  Why are you so far from helping me, from the words of my
    groaning?

O my God, I cry by day, but you do not answer;
   and by night, but find no rest.

Yet you are holy,
   enthroned on the praises of Israel.
In you our ancestors trusted;
   they trusted, and you delivered them.
To you they cried, and were saved;
   in you they trusted, and were not put to shame.

But I am a worm, and not human;
   scorned by others, and despised by the people.
All who see me mock at me; . . .
   they shake their heads;
"Commit your cause to the LORD; let him deliver—
   let him rescue the one in whom he delights!"

Yet it was you who took me from the womb;
   you kept me safe on my mother's breast.
On you I was cast from my birth,
   and since my mother bore me you have been my God.
Do not be far from me,
   for trouble is near
   and there is no one to help.

Many bulls encircle me,
   strong bulls of Bashan surround me;
they open wide their mouths at me,
   like a ravening and roaring lion.

I am poured out like water,
    and all my bones are out of joint;
my heart is like wax;
    it is melted within my breast;
my mouth is dried up like a potsherd,
    and my tongue sticks to my jaws;
    you lay me in the dust of death.

For dogs are all around me;
    a company of evildoers encircles me.
My hands and feet have shriveled;
I can count all my bones.
They stare and gloat over me;
they divide my clothes among themselves,
    and for my clothing they cast lots.

But you, O LORD, do not be far away!
    O my help, come quickly to my aid!
Deliver my soul from the sword,
    my life from the power of the dog!
    Save me from the mouth of the lion!

From the horns of the wild oxen you have rescued me.
I will tell of your name to my brothers and sisters;
    in the midst of the congregation I will praise you:
You who fear the LORD, praise him!
    All you offspring of Jacob, glorify him;
    stand in awe of him, all you offspring of Israel!
For he did not despise or abhor the affliction of the afflicted;
he did not hide his face from me,
    but heard when I cried to him.

From you comes my praise in the great congregation;
    my vows I will pay before those who fear him.
The poor shall eat and be satisfied;
    those who seek him shall praise the LORD.
    May your hearts live forever!
All the ends of the earth shall remember
    and turn to the LORD;
and all the families of the nations
    shall worship before him.
For dominion belongs to the LORD,
    and he rules over the nations.

To him, indeed, shall all who sleep in the earth bow down;
    before him shall bow all who go down to the dust,
    and I shall live for him.
Posterity will serve him;
    future generations will be told about the Lord,
and proclaim his deliverance to a people yet unborn,
    saying that he has done it.

- **Closing:**
  I let my heart speak simply and openly to Jesus.
  I pray the Our Father.

- **Review of Prayer:**
  I record in my journal the words and images of Psalm 22 that have most deeply touched me.

Into Your Hands
I Commend My Spirit

Week Six, Day 1 | Into Your Hands

Luke 23:44-46

> *It was now about noon, and darkness came over the whole land until three in the afternoon, while the sun's light failed; and the curtain of the temple was torn in two. Then Jesus, crying with a loud voice, said, "Father, into your hands I commend my spirit." Having said this, he breathed his last.*

Commentary

It is a terrible thing to fall into the hands of the living God (64, p. 239). It is an awful—awe-filled—experience to find oneself within the embrace of a love that asks of us all we are, yet gives to us a fullness of love that is humanly incomprehensible. Before the sheer mystery of such love, one is filled with reverence and fear.

On the cross, Jesus says yes to this love. The obedience to God that shaped Jesus' entire life climaxes in this final yes.

In spite of the intense physical suffering and aloneness he experiences, in spite of the human uncertainty of what death itself holds, Jesus says yes.

As the incomprehensibility of God looms frighteningly before him, the yes of Jesus is unconditional, total surrender. He surrenders his entire being, his whole person. He surrenders himself to one who, in spite of the incomprehensibility, Jesus can still address as "Father." Jesus lets go in love to the one who holds in love.

This love that releases Jesus into the presence of his Father releases power into our world. His yes is the evolutionary turning point of all creation. Through his surrender, the Temple veil that separates the presence of God from human experience is torn open.

Through Jesus the heart of God is made visible. We, as followers of Jesus, are given access to enter as he did into God's love and to find ourselves, like him, in the hands of love. Such love is, indeed, breathtaking!

Suggested Approach to Prayer: Prayer of Surrender

- **Daily Prayer Pattern:**
  I quiet myself and relax in the presence of God.
  I declare my dependence on God.

- **Grace:**
  I ask to enter deeply into the surrender of Jesus.

- **Method:** Repeated Prayer
  I take into my hands a cross or crucifix and fix my eyes upon it. I consider Jesus in his pain, as he is dying.

  I ask to be open to hear the prayer of Jesus as he prayed it. I ask to share his experience of this moment in his life, so that the surrender that shaped his prayer may resonate deeply within me.

  Gently and prayerfully, I allow the words of his prayer to become my own, as breathing in and out, I pray, "Father, into your hands I commend my spirit."

  I imagine myself passing through the torn curtain of the Temple, entering into the holiness of Jesus. In his presence I continue to pray his prayer of surrender: "Father, into your hands I commend my spirit."

- **Closing:**
  I speak to Christ simply, openly, offering to God my entire being.
  I pray the Our Father.

- **Review of Prayer:**
  I record in my journal the words of my offering, my surrender.

Week Six, Day 2 | Jesus Is Lord

Philippians 2:5-11

> *Let the same mind be in you that was in Christ Jesus,*
> *who, though he was in the form of God,*
> *did not regard equality with God*
> *as something to be exploited,*
> *but emptied himself,*
> *taking the form of a slave,*
> *being born in human likeness.*
> *And being found in human form,*
> *he humbled himself*
> *and became obedient to the point of death—*
> *even death on a cross.*
>
> *Therefore God also highly exalted him*
> *and gave him the name*
> *that is above every name,*
> *so that at the name of Jesus*
> *every knee should bend,*
> *in heaven and on earth and under the earth,*
> *and every tongue should confess*
> *that Jesus Christ is Lord,*
> *to the glory of God the Father.*

Commentary

When the spirit enters matter, matter becomes spirit. Jesus' surrender on the cross is the ultimate moment of his entry into our humanity. His dying is the definitive revelation of his incarnation. Who would dare imagine that in God's plan the wisdom that stretched "from one end of the earth to the other" (Wisdom 8:1) would be unveiled in this man on a cross? Who would dare imagine the ramifications of such a God-event?

Before the crucified Christ, our conception of God is turned upside down! The God of thunder and lightning (Exodus 19:16) hangs bound by nails. The God whose word unleashed the energies of creation (Genesis 1) is silent before his accusers. The God who is master of the universe is seen as servant of all (Isaiah 52:13–53:12).

This image of a humiliated, weak, and vulnerable God is difficult to accept and certainly unpopular. A God of power, intellect, and wealth is far more palatable. "Jews demand signs and Greeks desire wisdom, but we proclaim Christ crucified, a stumbling block to Jews and foolishness to Gentiles" (1 Corinthians 1:22-23).

Our God, however, will not be limited by our self-serving notions of divinity. God presents to us, in the humanity of Jesus, a totality of presence that touches the deepest recesses of incomprehensible love.

In Jesus we are presented with the loving vulnerability of God, a vulnerability that paradoxically contains within it all power. In Jesus we encounter God's own love-knowledge, which encompasses a wisdom that defies human articulation. In Jesus we are offered a servanthood that promises the entire community of believers an authentic royalty. "To those who are the called, . . ." we proclaim "Christ the power of God and the wisdom of God. For God's foolishness is wiser than human wisdom, and God's weakness is stronger than human strength" (1 Corinthians 1:24-25).

A new door has been opened! It provides an entry into a new mode of being. It is good news for those who choose to place their trust in the God of love, especially for those who poignantly experience their own wound-edness and poverty. And for those who have been snagged by pride, it is a chance to begin again.

The doorway to new life is the attitude of self-emptying that shaped the obedience of Jesus' life and death. Jesus does not call us to a self-emptying that is a repression or negation of the self. He calls us to a voluntary sur-render of power, a willingness to sink into the darkness of our own power-lessness and to encounter, within the negativity and void, the no-thingness that alone can reveal God.

Within this encounter with darkness, an option surfaces. One is unmer-cifully compelled to choose, to make the leap of surrender in trust and thereby opt for goodness, or failing, to remain fixated in indecision, an easy prey of evil.

Through the disobedience of the first Adam, we became divided and lim-ited. Now, through the self-emptying obedience of the new Adam, Jesus, the door to freedom and reconciliation has been opened to us.

Because Jesus crucified is Lord, not only has the way been opened, but we have been given access to the gift of God's love, the healing power that transforms our darkness. The human condition that God embraced in Jesus and that is our inheritance is most profoundly experienced in this surrendering leap of trust.

In self-emptying surrender, darkness gives way to light, and weakness is transformed into strength. Before such love we, as human creatures, can only kneel and proclaim with newfound joy, "Jesus is Lord."

Suggested Approach to Prayer: Jesus' Last Breath

• Daily Prayer Pattern:
   I quiet myself and relax in the presence of God.
   I declare my dependence on God.

- **Grace:**
  I ask to enter deeply into the spirit of Jesus' self-emptying surrender of love.

- **Method:** Contemplation
  I imagine myself at the foot of the cross of Jesus. I see his suffering culminating in short, excruciating gasps of breath. I see his chest expand as his lungs desperately strain for air. I see the pulse of his neck gradually weaken.

  I remain with Jesus in these last moments.

  I am aware of my feelings . . . of fear, desire to leave, sadness, regret, compassion, relief. I am aware of any memories of Jesus' life and my relationship with him. I call to mind experiences I have had when I knew the reality of his presence and his love within me. I become aware of any desires that surface within me—for example, to carry forward his mission . . . to reconcile with those I have wounded . . . to be faithful in the carrying of my own cross. . . .

  I continue to remain present in Jesus' final moments. I hear his final breath as he surrenders his spirit to God.

- **Closing:**
  I spend some moments in silence.
  I pray the Our Father.

- **Review of Prayer:**
  I record in my journal any insights or feelings that have surfaced during this period of prayer.

Week Six, Day 3 | Life and Spirit

John 19:31-37

> *Since it was the day of Preparation, the Jews did not want the bodies left on the cross during the sabbath, especially because that sabbath was a day of great solemnity. So they asked Pilate to have the legs of the crucified men broken and the bodies removed. Then the soldiers came and broke the legs of the first and of the other who had been crucified with him. But when they came to Jesus and saw that he was already dead, they did not break his legs. Instead, one of the soldiers pierced his side with a spear, and at once blood and water came out. (He who saw this has testified so that you also may believe. His testimony is true, and he knows that he tells the truth.) These things occurred so that the scripture might be fulfilled, "None of his bones shall be broken." And again another passage of scripture says, "They will look on the one whom they have pierced."*

Commentary

The lance that pierces the dead Jesus releases life and spirit. At the moment the soldier's lance penetrates Jesus' side, the heritage of the past and the legacy of Christ's risen Spirit converge and are materialized in the sign of blood and water.

A rich mosaic of words and images that sustained and gave direction to God's chosen people provides an understanding of the profound symbolism in this scene. The strongest Jewish scriptural image within this episode is the paschal lamb, whose blood marked the doorposts of the Hebrew people and saved them from the angel of death (Exodus 12:7-51). The blood of Jesus—the servant of Yahweh and the true paschal sacrifice—is the saving power for his people (Isaiah 53:6-7).

The ritual lamb had to be perfect, unblemished, and without any broken bones (Exodus 12:46); likewise, Jesus' body is spared the mutilation of the customary breaking of bones that was used to hasten death from crucifixion. The heart of the paschal lamb was slit open; the side of Jesus is pierced. Finally, Jesus dies at the very moment the lambs for Passover are being slaughtered in the temple.

The import of this moment is amplified by the fact that the temple of sacrifice was built upon the rock of Moriah, the site tradition identifies as the mountain to which Abraham brought his son Isaac to be sacrificed (Genesis 22:1-19). This rock of Abraham's sacrifice and the temple sacrifice, has given way to the life-giving sacrifice of Jesus on Mount Calvary.

The life-imparting effect of Jesus' blood (Deuteronomy 12:23-24), poured out for others, is beautifully symbolized in the life-giving water, sign of the Spirit. As Moses, in the dryness of the desert Passover (Exodus 17: 1-7), drew water from the rock, the people of the Christian Scriptures draw water from Jesus, the "spiritual rock" (1 Corinthians 10:4). And Jesus says, "Let anyone who is thirsty come to me." (John 7:37).

Suggested Approach to Prayer: Lamb of God

• **Daily Prayer Pattern:**
  I quiet myself and relax in the presence of God.
  I declare my dependence on God.

• **Grace:**
  I ask to share deeply in the life and spirit of Jesus crucified.

- **Method:** Contemplation

I imagine myself at the foot of the cross. I see the dead body of Jesus hanging limply on the cross. I become as totally present as I can before Jesus.

I hear the soldiers approach and see them break the bones of those others who have been crucified with Jesus. I see a soldier approach Jesus, and I note his awareness that Jesus is already dead. I see him plunge his lance into Jesus' side. I see the blood and water flow from the wound.

I remain before Jesus, quiet within. Intermittently I pray interiorly the following: "Lamb of God, you take way the sins of the world: have mercy on me."

- **Closing:**

I say openly and simply to Christ whatever arises within me.
I pray the Our Father.

- **Review of Prayer:**

I record in my journal whatever insights and feelings have surfaced during this time of prayer.

Week Six, Day 4 | A Royal Burial

John 19:38-42

> *After these things, Joseph of Arimathea, who was a disciple of Jesus, though a secret one because of his fear of the Jews, asked Pilate to let him take away the body of Jesus. Pilate gave him permission; so he came and removed his body. Nicodemus, who had at first come to Jesus by night, also came, bringing a mixture of myrrh and aloes, weighing about a hundred pounds. They took the body of Jesus and wrapped it with the spices in linen cloths, according to the burial custom of the Jews. Now there was a garden in the place where he was crucified, and in the garden there was a new tomb in which no one had ever been laid.*
>
> *And so, because it was the Jewish day of Preparation, and the tomb was nearby, they laid Jesus there.*

Commentary

Jesus was crowned a king; he was hailed and enthroned and proclaimed a king! True, his crown was one of thorns, his throne a cross, and mockery his royal acclamation. Nonetheless, he is a king!

In his burial, the kingship previously denied Jesus in life is outwardly acknowledged. Inevitably the inner reality of Christ's kingship finally received a more fitting external expression. What was hidden comes to light.

Jesus' burial is lavish! He is given a "tomb with the rich" (Isaiah 53:9), a new tomb surrounded by a private garden enclosure. The amount of spices with which his body is prepared is extraordinary, and the burial recalls the royal entombment of ancient kings (Nehemiah 3:16).

Interestingly, the generosity of two believers—Joseph of Arimathaea and Nicodemus, who up to the time of Jesus' death had remained secret believers—makes visible the truth of Jesus' kingship. Joseph and Nicodemus show that even in the Sanhedrin and among the hostile Jewish opposition some believed in Jesus, yet remained silent because they feared ridicule and rejection. Now, when many of Jesus' disciples have fled in fear, Joseph and Nicodemus come forward.

Even in the ultimate weakness of death, Jesus empowers the weak. Who but the weak and hidden can recognize a king who is weak and whose kingship is invisible?

It is the weak and the fearful among us (and within us) who, like Joseph and Nicodemus, see and claim in Christ the life and power of his kingship. In the recognition and claiming of the power of Christ, weakness becomes strength. "And your life is hidden with Christ in God. When Christ who is your life is revealed, then you also will be revealed with him in glory" (Colossians 3:3b-4).

Suggested Approach to Prayer: A New Tomb

- **Daily Prayer Pattern:**
  I quiet myself and relax in the presence of God.
  I declare my dependence on God.

- **Grace:**
  I ask for the gift of a passionate love for Christ, a love that will sustain me in life and death.

- **Method:** Contemplation

I imagine myself entering Jesus' tomb, and I am aware of its deep silence. I stand before Jesus, who is prepared for burial. I contemplate his still, lifeless body. I see the white linen bands in which his body is wrapped. I am aware of the aroma of the spices and the fragrance of the oils that were used to anoint him.

Looking outside the tomb, I consider meditatively the beauty of its garden enclosure, the freshness of the newly cut rock, and the extraordinary fragrance that surrounds me.

I consider this man who was crucified in weakness and now buried in such splendor. I remain quietly in prayer.

- **Closing:**

I allow my heart to speak to Jesus, thanking him for his great love and asking him to further reveal to me the meaning of this event. I close my prayer by rereading Colossians 3:3b-4.

- **Review of Prayer:**

I note in my journal whatever feelings and insights have surfaced during my prayer period.

Week Six, Day 5 | Repetition

Suggested Approach to Prayer

- **Daily Prayer Pattern:**
  I quiet myself and relax in the presence of God.
  I declare my dependence on God.

- **Grace:**
  I ask for the gift of a deepening share of the self-emptying, surrendering love that sustained and moved Jesus to live and to die for us.

- **Method:** Repetition
  Because of the importance of reflecting on these past weeks of praying about Jesus' passion, you may want to spend several days meditatively rereading your prayer journal.

  In addition, spend one or more periods of prayer allowing the effect of Christ's death to permeate your being and enabling you to further see its energy, like light, spreading out and filling the world.

- **Review of Prayer:**
  I write in my journal any feelings, experiences, or insights that have surfaced.

Week Six, Day 6 | Labors of Love

Isaiah 52:13–53:12

See, my servant shall prosper; he shall be exalted and lifted up, and shall be very high. Just as there were many who were astonished at him—so marred was his appearance, beyond human semblance, and his form beyond that of mortals—so he shall startle many nations; kings shall shut their mouths because of him; for that which had not been told them they shall see, and that which they had not heard they shall contemplate.

Who has believed what we have heard? And to whom has the arm of the LORD been revealed? For he grew up before him like a young plant, and like a root out of dry ground; he had no form or majesty that we should look at him, nothing in his appearance that we should desire him. He was despised and rejected by others; a man of suffering and acquainted with infirmity; and as one from whom others hide their faces he was despised, and we held him of no account.

Surely he has borne our infirmities and carried our diseases; yet we accounted him stricken, struck down by God, and afflicted. But he was wounded for our transgressions, crushed for our iniquities; upon him was the punishment that made us whole, and by his bruises we are healed. All we like sheep have gone astray; we have all turned to our own way, and the LORD has laid on him the iniquity of us all.

He was oppressed, and he was afflicted, yet he did not open his mouth; like a lamb that is led to the slaughter, and like a sheep that before its shearers is silent, so he did not open his mouth. By a perversion of justice he was taken away. Who could have imagined his future? For he was cut off from the land of the living, stricken for the transgression of my people. They made his grave with the wicked and his tomb with the rich, although he had done no violence, and there was no deceit in his mouth.

Yet it was the will of the LORD *to crush him with pain. When you make his life an offering for sin, he shall see his offspring, and shall prolong his days; through him the will of the* LORD *shall prosper. Out of his anguish he shall see light; he shall find satisfaction through his knowledge. The righteous one, my servant, shall make many righteous, and he shall bear their iniquities. Therefore I will allot him a portion with the great, and he shall divide the spoil with the strong; because he poured out himself to death, and was numbered with the transgressors; yet he bore the sin of many, and made intercession for the transgressors.*

Commentary

In spite of all the energy we expend trying not to suffer, we do suffer. In spite of all the effort we make to blind ourselves to the sufferings of others, we see their pain. Not only do we observe suffering in others and personally experience it ourselves, but also we somehow receive an inner sense of goodness and growth from suffering.

No doubt, suffering is a mysterious, compelling, human reality.

The earliest, and probably the most profound, statement on human suffering in all of literature is the Song of the Suffering Servant found in the Book of Isaiah. In his writing, Isaiah, one of the greatest prophets and poets of the Jewish Scriptures, brought to the Jewish people a message of their deliverance from bondage by a God of tender compassion. It is a message of hope for a displaced people who have undergone the total collapse of their nation, the loss of their religious center, and utter homelessness in a land of exile. In words that transcend his own time and nation, Isaiah attempted to lead his people to discover, within their suffering, a new meaning that would carry them into the future.

The song depicts an ideal servant of Yahweh. The role of the servant is to liberate others by willingly and consciously taking upon himself or herself their pain, sin, and suffering. While this message of Isaiah never inspired great enthusiasm among his Jewish compatriots, it does hold for humanity the way to utilize and transform the ever-present reality of human suffering.

Jesus consistently identified with and lived out of the spirit of the suffering servant of Isaiah (Mark 8:31; Matthew 17:22-23; Luke 18:31-34). As God's beloved Son (Isaiah 42:1), Jesus provides us with the model for suffering and the means of true servanthood through his life, his cross, and his resurrection. He empowers us to realize our own true identity and destiny in the evolutionary process of the world toward oneness in him.

As creative agents of Christ, actively involved in moving the world forward, we are called to three specific tasks, to three labors of love (27, pp. 82–83). Teilhard de Chardin speaks of these three tasks as an interconnected dynamic process and calls them centration, decentration, and surcentration. The tasks correspond to the threefold dynamic of the paschal mystery: the life, death, and resurrection of Jesus.

The first task (life) is to develop ourselves, to foster self-knowledge, integration, and Christian maturity. It is to embrace in trust and surrender whatever gifts or limitations we may encounter on this journey inward.

The second task (death) flows from and complements the first. It is to extend ourselves to others in compassion, whatever their need or pain. This extension entails the hard labor of caring for others when there is no reciprocation. It means forgiving unconditionally, that is, without retaliation. It may even involve, on occasion, deliberately allowing ourselves to encounter the evil in others and to overcome it through the power of love. This second task is a call to decisively choose the common good, which includes a predilection for the poor and the weak among us, those who are shunned and rejected, lost and unattractive.

This extension of self means that when we personally suffer, we remain open to the possibility that our suffering is being mysteriously used to bring healing to others. This second task of loving is, in the truest sense, a work of unification, the laying down of one's life for others.

The first and second tasks give rise to the third task (resurrection), which is to allow oneself to be shaped by the working of the Spirit within, rather than to be driven by egotistical desires or compulsive perfectionism. It is to become Christ-centered through a total surrender of our lives to God.

In the Song of the Suffering Servant we hear the spirit and prayer of Jesus as he surrenders to the love that has forever transformed the deepest yearning of our hearts. In the words of the fathers of the Second Vatican Council,

> Such is the mystery of humankind, and it is a great one, as seen by believers in the light of Christian revelation. Through Christ and in Christ, the riddles of sorrow and death grow meaningful. Apart from his gospel, they overwhelm us. Christ has risen, destroying death by His death. He has lavished life upon us so that, as sons and daughters in the Son, we can cry out in the Spirit: Abba! (1, *The Church in the Modern World*, 22, p. 222)

Suggested Approach to Prayer: Servant of the Spirit

- **Daily Prayer Pattern:**
  I quiet myself and relax in the presence of God.
  I declare my dependence on God.

- **Grace:**
  I ask to enter deeply, fully, into the Spirit of Jesus' self-emptying, surrendering love.

- **Method:** Meditative Reading
  In stillness I approach the servant song of Isaiah. Slowly I read the words of Isaiah, quietly aware of the gifts that have been given to me as I prayerfully walked with Jesus through his passion.

  As I make my way prayerfully through the song, verse by verse, I am receptive to the powerful images of the servant. I allow these images to take on form and shape within me.

  If any image particularly resonates within me, I stay with it, drawing from it whatever consolation or insight it nurtures.

  Focusing on the theme of the song, through suffering to glory, I enter into the spirit of the servant. Prayerfully, I reflect on Jesus coming into his glory.

- **Closing:**
  I speak to Christ, heart-to-heart, of my thanks to him and my desire to live in his Spirit.
  I close by praying the prayer Soul of Christ, on p. 164.

- **Review of Prayer:**
  I write my own offering and commitment to Christ.

Appendix 1: Additional Prayers

Soul of Christ

Jesus, may all that is you flow into me.
May your body and blood be my food and drink.
May your passion and death be my strength and life.
Jesus, with you by my side enough has been given.
May the shelter I seek be the shadow of your cross.
Let me not run from the love which you offer,
    but hold me safe from the forces of evil.
On each of my dyings shed your light and your love.
Keep calling to me until that day comes,
    when with your saints, I may praise you forever.

(31, p. 3)

Letting Go

To a dear one about whom I have been concerned.
I behold the Christ in you.
I place you lovingly in the care of the Father.
I release you from my anxiety and concern.
I let go of my possessive hold on you.
I am willing to free you to follow the dictates
    of your indwelling Lord.
I am willing to free you to live your life
    according to your best light and understanding.
Husband, wife, child, friend—
I no longer try to force my ideas on you,
    my ways on you.

I lift my thoughts above you, above the personal level.
I see you as God sees you, a spiritual being, created
   in his image, and endowed with qualities and abilities
   that make you needed, and important—not only to me but
   to God and His larger plan.
I do not bind you, I no longer believe that you do not have
   the understanding you need in order to meet life.
I bless you.
   I have faith in you.
      I behold Jesus in you.

(Author unknown; 73, p. 100)

Prayer of Hope for the World

Lord God, we come to you in our need; create in us an awareness of
   the massive and seemingly irreversible proportions of the crisis we face
   today and a sense of urgency to activate the forces of goodness.
Where there is blatant nationalism, let there be a global, universal
   concern;
Where there is war and armed conflict, let there be negotiation;
Where there is stockpiling, let there be disarmament;
Where people struggle toward liberation, let there be noninterference;
Where there is consumerism, let there be a care to preserve the earth's
   resources;
Where there is abundance, let there be a choice for a simple lifestyle and
   sharing;
Where there is reliance on external activism, let there be a balance of
   prayerful dependence on you, O Lord;
Where there is selfish individualism, let there be an openness to
   community;

Where there is the sin of injustice, let there be guilt, confession, and
    atonement;
Where there is paralysis and numbness before the enormity of the
    problems, let there be confidence in our collective effort.

Lord, let us not so much be concerned to be cared for as to care, not so
much to be materially secure as to know that we are loved by you. Let
us not look to be served, but to place ourselves at the service of others
whatever cost to self-interest, for it is in loving vulnerability that we, like
Jesus, experience the fullness of what it means to be human. And it is in
serving that we discover the healing springs of life that will bring about a
new birth to our earth and hope to our world. Amen. (11, pp. 7–8)

Appendix 2: For Spiritual Directors

The passages and commentaries in this guide are keyed to the *Spiritual Exercises of Saint Ignatius*. The number in parentheses indicates the numbered paragraph as found in the original text.

For "The Principle and Foundation," see *Love*, Take and Receive series. For Week 1, see *Forgiveness*; for Week 2, see *Birth* and the following:

Week II

(284) Luke 9:28-36 Inexpressible Joy
Eleventh Day (161)
(285) John 11:1-44 Awakening
(286) John 12:1-8 Anointed with Love
Twelfth Day (162)
(287) Matthew 21:1-17 He Who Comes

Week III

First Day (190–207)
(289) John 13:1-16 A Basin, Some Water, and a Towel
     Luke 22:14-23 In Remembrance
     John 17:1-26 The Secret Place, the Sacred Place
(290) Mark 14:32-42 Out of the Darkness
     Matthew 6:9b-13 Abba—Our Father
Second Day (208)
(291) Matthew 26:47-56 The Kiss
(292) Luke 22:54-65 The Night Before
     Luke 22:66—23:1 The Bound Prisoner
Third Day
(293) Matthew 27:11-25 Suffered under Pontius Pilate
(294) Luke 23:6-12 Silent before Herod

Fourth Day

(295) John 18:33-38; 19:1-12 Truth on Trial

Fifth Day

(296) John 19:13-22 Good Friday Journey

John 19:23-24 King and Priest

Luke 23:39-43 Stretched between Opposites

(297) John 19:25-27 From Mother to Woman

John 19:28-29 One of Us

Matthew 27:39-44 The Cross—Catalyst

Matthew 27:45-40 Cry of Distress

Luke 23:44-46 Into Your Hands

Philippians 2:5-11 Jesus is Lord

John 19:31-37 Life and Spirit

Sixth Day

(298) John 19:38-42 A Royal Burial

Seventh Day

Repetition

Isaiah 52:13–53:12 Labors of Love

Appendix 3: Approaches to Prayer

Week 1: Day 1 Luke 9:23-27   Personal Invitation (contemplation)
        Day 2 Luke 9:28-36   The Enveloping Cloud (contemplation)
        Day 3 John 11:1-44   "Come Out" (contemplation)
        Day 4 John 11:45-54 Response to Jesus (contemplation)
        Day 5 John 12:1-8   The Fragrance of Presence (contemplation)
Week 2: Day 1 Matthew 21:1-17   The Man on the Donkey
                                  (contemplation)
        Day 2 John 12:23-32   My Tree (contemplation)
        Day 3 John 13:1-16   Bathed in Love (contemplation)
        Day 4 Luke 22:14-23   At the Table (contemplation)
        Day 5 John 17:1-26   The Mind and Heart of Jesus (meditative
                              reading)
Week 3: Day 1 Mark 14:32-42   Into the Garden (contemplation)
        Day 2 Matthew 6:9b-13   Our Father (meditative reading)
        Day 3 Matthew 26:47-56 Night of Betrayal (contemplation)
        Day 4 Luke 22:54-65   The Look of Jesus (contemplation)
        Day 5 Luke 22:66–23:1   Lord Jesus Christ (repeated prayer)
Week 4: Day 1 Matthew 27:11-25   The Creed (meditative reading)
        Day 2 Luke 23:6-12   Entry into Silence (contemplation)
        Day 3 John 18:33-38; 19:1-12   Jesus, Mocked and Rejected
                                        (contemplation)
        Day 4 John 19:13-22   The Way of the Cross (meditation)
        Day 5 John 19:23-24   Before the Cross (contemplation and
                              repeated prayer)
Week 5: Day 1 Luke 23:39-43   Promise of Paradise (contemplation)
        Day 2 John 19:25-27   Prayer of Mary (repeated prayer)
        Day 3 John 19:28-29   I Thirst (meditation)

Day 4 Matthew 27:39-44   The Heart of Christ
(contemplation)
Day 6 Matthew 27:45-50   Psalm 22 (meditative reading)
Week 6: Day 1 Luke 23:44-46   Surrender (repeated prayer)
Day 2 Philippians 2:5-11   Jesus' Last Breath (contemplation)
Day 3 John 19:31-37   Lamb of God (contemplation and
repeated prayer)
Day 4 John 19:38-42   A New Tomb (contemplation)
Day 6 Isaiah 52:13–53:12   Servant of the Spirit (meditative
reading)

Bibliography

1. Abbot, Walter M., ed. *The Documents of Vatican II*. New York: American Press, 1966.
2. Albright, W.F., and C.S. Mann. *Matthew*. Garden City, NY: Doubleday & Co., 1971.
3. Alighieri, Dante. *The Divine Comedy*. New York: Rinehart and Co., Inc., 1954.
4. Anderson, Bernard W. *Understanding the Old Testament*. Englewood Cliffs, NJ: Prentice-Hall, 1975.
5. Barclay, William. *The Gospel of John*. Vol. 2. Philadelphia: Westminster Press, 1975.
6. Barclay. *The Gospel of Luke*. Philadelphia: Westminster Press, 1975.
7. Barclay. *The Gospel of Mark*. Philadelphia: Westminster Press, 1975.
8. Barclay. *The Gospel of Matthew*. vol. 1, vol. 2. Philadelphia: Westminster Press, 1975.
9. Barclay. *The Letters to the Philippians, Colossians, and Thessalonians*. Philadelphia: Westminster Press, 1975.
10. Benoit, Pierre. *The Passion and Resurrection of Jesus Christ*. New York: Herder and Herder, 1969.
11. Bergan, Jacqueline, and Marie Schwan. *Peace*. Privately printed, 1983.
12. Bernstein, Leonard. *Kaddish*. Symphony No. 3, Columbia Recording.
13. Bridges, Robert, ed. *Poems of Gerard Manley Hopkins*. New York: Oxford University Press, 1948.
14. Brown, Raymond. *A Crucified Christ in Holy Week*. Collegeville, MN: The Liturgical Press, 1986.
15. Brown. *The Gospel According to John XII–XXI*. Garden City, NY: Doubleday & Co., 1966.

16. Brown, et al. *The Jerome Biblical Commentary*. Englewood Cliffs, NJ: Prentice-Hall, 1968.

17. Brueggemann, Walter. *The Prophetic Imagination*. Philadelphia: Fortress Press, 1978.

18. Caird, G. B. *Saint Luke*. London: Penguin Books, 1963.

19. Cowan, Marian, and John C. Futrell. *The Spiritual Exercises of St. Ignatius of Loyola: A Handbook for Directors*. New York: Le Jacq Publishing, 1982.

20. Crossman, Dominic M. "The Gospel of Jesus Christ." Stonebridge Priory, Lake Bluff, IL. Mimeographed notes, 1963.

21. de Mello, Anthony. *Sadhana, A Way to God*. Saint Louis: The Institute of Jesuit Sources, 1978.

22. de Mello. *Wellsprings*. Garden City, NY: Doubleday & Co., 1985.

23. Doore, Gary. "The Dynamics of Transformation," *The American Theosophist*. 74 (May 1986).

24. Eliade, Mircea. *The Sacred and the Profane*. New York: Harcourt, Brace & World, Inc., 1957.

25. English, John. *Choosing Life*. New York: Paulist Press, 1978.

26. English. *Spiritual Freedom*. Guelph, Ontario: Loyola House, 1974.

27. Faricy, Robert. *The Spirituality of Teilhard de Chardin*. Minneapolis: Winston Press, 1981.

28. Fenton, J. C. *Saint Matthew*. London: Penguin Books, 1963.

29. Fitzmyer, Joseph. *The Gospel According to Luke X-XXIV*. Garden City, NY: Doubleday & Co., 1985.

30. Fleming, David. *Draw Me Into Your Friendship: A Literal Translation and a Contemporary Reading of the Spiritual Exercises*. Saint Louis: The Institute of Jesuit Sources, 1978.

31. Fox, Matthew. *Breakthrough*. Garden City, NY: Image Books, 1977.

32. Fox. *Original Blessing*. Santa Fe, NM: Bear and Co., 1983.

33. Getty, Mary Ann. *Philippians and Philemon*. Wilmington, DE: Michael Glazier, 1980.

34. Gill, Jean. *Images of My Self*. New York: Paulist Press, 1982.
35. Gibran, Kahlil. *Lazarus and His Beloved*. Greenwood, CT: New York Graphic Society, Ltd., 1973.
36. Harrington, Wilfred. *Mark*. Wilmington, DE: Michael Glazier, 1979.
37. Harriot, John. "Himself He Cannot Save." *The Way*. 10 (October 1970): 318-326.
38. John Paul II. *On the Christian Meaning of Suffering*. Washington, DC: USCC, 1984.
39. Jung, Carl G. *Aion*. Princeton, NJ: Princeton University Press, 1959.
40. Jung. *Man and His Symbols*. New York: Valor Publication, 1964.
41. Jung. *The Visions Seminars*, Book 1, 2. Switzerland: Spring Publications, 1976.
42. Küng, Hans. *On Being a Christian*. Garden City, NY: Doubleday & Co., 1976.
43. La Verdiere, Eugene. *Luke*. Wilmington, DE: Michael Glazier, 1980.
44. Luke, Helen M. *Woman: Earth and Spirit*. New York: Crossroads, 1985.
45. McBrien, Richard P. *Catholicism*, Vol. 1, 2. Minneapolis: Winston Press, 1980.
46. McGann, Diarmuid. *The Journeying Self*. New York: Paulist Press, 1985.
47. McKenzie, John. *Dictionary of the Bible*. Milwaukee: Bruce Publishing Co., 1965.
48. McKenzie. *Second Isaiah*. Garden City, NY: Doubleday & Co., 1968.
49. McPalin, James. *John*. Wilmington, DE: Michael Glazier, 1979.
50. Magaña, José. *A Strategy for Liberation*. Hicksville, NY: Exposition Press, 1974.
51. Marsh, John. *St. John*. London: Penguin Books, 1968.
52. Meier, John P. *Matthew*. Wilmington, DE: Michael Glazier, 1980.

53. Moltmann, Jürgen, and Johann Metz. *Meditations on the Passion*. New York: Paulist Press, 1979.

54. National Conference of Catholic Bishops. *The Sacramentary*. New York: Catholic Books Publishing Co., 1974.

55. Neumann, Erick. *The Great Mother*. Princeton, NJ: Princeton University Press, 1963.

56. Nineham, D.E. *Mark*. Baltimore: Penguin Books, 1963.

57. Oesterreicher, John M. ed. *The Bridge*. New York: Pantheon Books, 1955.

58. O'Neill, Eugene. "Lazarus Laughed," *The Plays of Eugene O'Neill*. New York: Random House, 1954. 273-376.

59. Paoli, Arturo. *Freedom to be Free*. Maryknoll, NY: Orbis Books, 1973.

60. Peck, M. Scott. *People of the Lie*. New York: Simon & Schuster, Inc., 1983.

61. Pennington, M. Basil. *Centering Prayer*. Garden City, NY: Image Books, 1982.

62. Perkins, Pheme. *Resurrection*. Garden City, NY: Doubleday & Co., 1984.

63. Rahner, Karl. *Foundations of Christian Faith*. New York: The Seabury Press, 1978.

64. Rahner. *Spiritual Exercises*. New York: Herder and Herder, 1956.

65. Rollings, Wayne G. *Jung and the Bible*. Atlanta: John Knox Press, 1983.

66. Sanford, John A. *The Kingdom Within*. New York: Paulist Press, 1970.

67. Scullion, John. *Isaiah 40-66*. Wilmington, DE: Michael Glazier, 1982.

68. Stanley, David M. *A Modern Spiritual Approach to the Spiritual Exercises*. St. Louis: The Institute of Jesuit Sources, 1971.

69. Tannehill, Robert C. *A Mirror for Disciples: A Study of the Gospel of Mark*. Nashville, TN: Disciples Resources, 1977.
70. Taylor, Vincent. *The Gospel According to St. Mark*. New York: St. Martin's Press, 1966.
71. Teilhard de Chardin, Pierre. *The Divine Milieu*. New York: Harper and Row, 1966.
72. Ulanov, Ann and Barry. *Primary Speech: A Psychology of Prayer*. Atlanta: John Knox Press, 1982.
73. Veltri, John. *Orientations, Vol. 1: A Collection of Helps for Prayer*. Guelph, Ontario: Loyola House, 1979.
74. Veltri. *Orientations, Vol. 2, Annotation 19: Tentative Edition*. Guelph, Ontario: Loyola House, 1981.
75. von Franz, Marie-Louise. *Interpretation of Fairy Tales*. Dallas: Spring Publications, 1982.
76. von le Fort, Gertrud. *The Wife of Pilate*. Milwaukee: Bruce Publishing Co., 1957.
77. Welch, John. *Spiritual Pilgrims*. New York: Paulist Press, 1982.
78. Whitmont, Edward. *Return of the Goddess*. New York: Crossroads, 1984.
79. Woodman, Marion. *Addiction to Perfection*. Toronto: Inner City Books, 1982.
80. Woodman. *The Pregnant Virgin*. Toronto: Inner City Books, 1985.

About the Authors

In 1976, under the auspices of the Center for Christian Renewal, Jacqueline Syrup Bergan and Marie Schwan, CSJ, began a ministry together of providing days of prayer for parishes in northwestern Minnesota. Out of their own love and appreciation for the *Spiritual Exercises of St. Ignatius*, they began to write the Take and Receive series as a way of responding to the spiritual hunger of the people to whom they ministered.

Jacqueline, a wife, mother, and grandmother, has always had a keen interest in spirituality. She and her husband, Leonard, live in Minnesota for part of the year and spend the remainder of their time in Arizona.

Marie is a Sister of St. Joseph of Medaille. A teacher by profession, she has served in administration and formation in her congregation, and has recently completed fourteen years as associate director of Jesuit Retreat House in Oshkosh, Wisconsin. She is currently formation director for her community in New Orleans, Louisiana.